PERCY THROWER

By the same author

Thomas Hardy
Julian Hodge
Pope John Paul II
The Papal Visit
The English Country House
(with Mark Girouard and Fred Maroon)

PERCY THROWER
—————— A BIOGRAPHY ——————

TIMOTHY O'SULLIVAN

SIDGWICK & JACKSON
LONDON

First published in Great Britain in 1989 by
Sidgwick & Jackson Limited

All photographs are reproduced by kind permission of
Mrs Connie Thrower, except where otherwise indicated

The author and publishers gratefully acknowledge Mrs Roy
Plomley, Mrs Connie Thrower and BBC Radio for
permission to use the quote from *Desert Island Discs* which
appears on pp. 107–9, and the Hamlyn Publishing Group
Limited for the extracts taken from *In Your Garden with Percy
Thrower* which appear on pp. 126–134 and p. 137 and *Percy
Thrower's Every Day Gardening in Colour* which appear on
pp. 134–8

ISBN 0-283-99800-8

Photoset by Rowland Phototypesetting Limited
Bury St Edmunds, Suffolk
Printed in Great Britain by
Mackays of Chatham plc, Chatham, Kent
for Sidgwick & Jackson Limited
1 Tavistock Chambers, Bloomsbury Way
London WC1A 2SG

To
Paris and Zephyr

Fortunatus et ille deos qui novit agrestis

Contents

Acknowledgements

In the course of a discussion of the Royal Household, some years after I had met Percy Thrower, Carey Smith, of Sidgwick & Jackson, suggested that I write a biography of Percy. My first debt is therefore to Carey Smith for asking me to write the book and for her patience and imaginative interest in it while I was at work.

I am very much indebted to Mrs Connie Thrower for talking to me at considerable length about her husband, herself, their family and his work. I am also grateful to her for kindly lending most of the photographs used in this book.

Peter Road-Night, Secretary of the Shropshire Horticultural Society, kindly lent me some tapes of Percy talking in 1985 about himself and gardening in general. Some of the anecdotes on the tapes were told in a manner that was highly polished, even by Percy's standards, and I suspect that he had been dining out on them for years. Nevertheless, they seemed worth repeating here to a wider audience. I am similarly indebted to Barrie Edgar, probably the longest serving of Percy's television producers, for lending me his scrap-books and some video recordings.

A letter in several newspapers and gardening periodicals produced about four hundred variously interesting replies. I am particularly indebted to the following for their assistance with information, whether by letter or in conversation: Lord Aberconway, Sir David Attenborough, Mary Baker, Godfrey

Baseley, Brian Bass, M. J. Beardall (Principal Leisure Services Officer, Shrewsbury and Atcham Borough Council), the Hon Nicholas Beaumont, Arthur Billitt, Mrs Evelyn Brooks, Ken Brown, A. H. Burch, Paul Chaffens, John Cowell (Secretary, Royal Horticultural Society), Gerald Cox (Deputy Librarian, *The Daily Telegraph*), Doug Craddock, Mrs Arthur Deadman, Bill Duncalf, C. East (Editor, *Bucks Advertiser*), T. H. A. Edes, Eric Flounders, Mrs Jean Forrest, John Furness, Mrs Joan Garton, D. E. Gay, Mrs Karen Goring, Lt-Col K. J. Grapes (Secretary, Royal National Rose Society), Marian Halford (Archivist, Shropshire County Council), A. G. Hall, Geoffrey Hall, Janice Hall, Mrs May Hammond, Mrs Lena Hasell, Sir Francis Head, Charles Heady, Arthur Hellyer, Ken Hodgkinson, J. P. Hopkinson, Mrs Sheila Hull, A. E. Jakeman (Library, Foreign and Commonwealth Office), Shirley Jenever, Peter Konig, Russell Lewis, Alex Leys (Editor, *Derby Evening Telegraph*), Roddy Llewellyn, James Lloyd, Mrs I. McCabe (Librarian, The Royal Institution), Mrs M. Mannion, Mrs Daphne Melton, Elspeth Napier (Editor, *The Garden*), the late Duke of Northumberland, Stuart Ogg, Mary Owen, Sue Page, Mrs Roy Plomley, the Revd Prebendary Michael Pollit, Sir George Porter, Peter Pritchett-Brown, Jane Reynolds, Mrs B. Richardson, J. R. Rogers, Sam Rogers, Miss Rachel Salt, Peter Seabrook, Mrs Maude Seaton, Mrs Betty Smale, Neil Somerville and Jeff Walden (BBC Written Archives), G. Spate (Assistant Director, Leisure Services, City of Derby), Maurice Thrower, the Revd Maurice Turner, Michael Unger (Editor, *Manchester Evening News*), Brian Ward, Mrs Elizabeth Ward, N. K. Whetstone (Editor, *Birmingham Post*), Mrs Marjorie Whitaker, Ken White, Doug Whittingham, Alan Wilding, John Wilkie, John Williams, and R. Williams (Editor, *Shrewsbury Chronicle*).

Finally, for highly congenial hospitality while writing the book, it is a pleasure to thank: Judy Coleridge, Virginia Gasper, Richard Perceval Graves, John Haffenden, Neil and Christine Hamilton, Peter Hopkins, Gillian and Kevin O'Sullivan, Barbara Ozieblo-Rajkowska, and Brian and Brenda Sanctuary.

Timothy O'Sullivan

Rye
East Sussex
December 1988

Preface

I met Percy Thrower once – during the summer of 1977, I think. A retired part-time gardener of my mother's, Robert Scott, had been a friend since Percy's days at Windsor in the early 1930s, and when Percy was back in the area he would occasionally come and see him. Scott was proud of my mother's garden, though it was not of his making, and one day brought Percy round to see it. The garden was in a lush and enervating spot close to the Thames at Datchet and had been designed, in so far as it had been designed at all, for scent and to give an illusion of size. Within its limits of rather less than an acre it was quite a success. Percy made his way around the garden and came to a stop beside the Bourbon 'Louise Odier', which I regret to say was showing signs of mildew, sniffed, and gave a brisk lecture on the control of mildew. I do not think the garden was particularly to Percy's taste.

It was typical of Scott not to introduce us; but although Percy had been off the screen as presenter of *Gardeners' World* for more than a year, it was hardly necessary to be told who he was. If I had not known, I might have assumed from his appearance and confident, affable manner that he was the managing director of a fungicide manufacturer approaching, though definitely some years away from, retirement. Other surprises beside the figure with whom I was familiar on television were the speed with which he moved and thought. He moved in short, quick, precise steps and negotiated the

xiii

labyrinth of my mother's garden with very little guidance, clearly taking in far more than he chose to comment on. There were no 'ums' or 'ers' in his conversation. My impression was of one wholly and happily absorbed in his work, possibly to the exclusion of everything else, and happy to talk to anyone who happened to share that interest.

Part of the pleasure and privilege of writing this book has been to discover, usually from people who knew Percy far better than I did, that the impression he made on me in a few minutes was close to the impression formed by them after friendships which in a few instances had been lifelong. This is not to suggest that he had seemed at all shallow, but rather that he gave the whole of himself very freely and directly. He had a thoroughly positive attitude towards any job or circumstance which was perhaps rooted in the days when he worked in the highly disciplined world of a country house garden, where any work not done properly would be ordered to be done again until it was perfect. He took this habit of perfection with him into the limelight, to the approval of his audiences and colleagues alike. 'It was a real pleasure to work with such a professional,' Bill Duncalf, one of his producers on *Gardeners' World*, told me. 'He always got his lines and his work right first time.'

In a way, this total commitment to the job in hand is no more than the hallmark of anyone who excels in any occupation. In Percy's case his commitments were so many and his days, until the last two or three months of his life, so full, that he had little opportunity to look back. Nor, in the course of writing this book, did I discover in him any inclination to reflect on the past. His only admitted recreation, apart from gardening, was the active and generally very sociable sport of shooting. He could not understand anyone who would want to spend time fishing. On his early morning reconnaissances of the Quarry at Shrewsbury he would see fishermen in all weathers hunched on the banks of the Severn and recalled thinking that they must 'have difficult wives or come from unhappy homes or something'. The crisp, efficient tone of his memoirs (*My Lifetime of Gardening*, 1977), though eloquent of one side of the man, are a strong invitation to any biographer.

1

Horwood House

Little Horwood in Buckinghamshire, where Percy Thrower was born on 30 January 1913, has a better claim than most places to call itself the geographical middle of England. Buckinghamshire, one of the smallest English counties, is also one of the most varied, ranging from the lush country along the River Thames which for much of Percy's lifetime was nobly ornamented with elms, to the harsher, broader uplands on the Northamptonshire border. Over much of the middle of the county the heavy Oxford Clay was relatively late in being brought into cultivation and settlement was consequently thin. Medieval Buckinghamshire had no cathedral, no substantial monastery, no castle of the first rank, nor even many fortified manor houses. Buckinghamshire's prosperity came with the eighteenth century and the ordering of the landscape into neat, hawthorn-edged fields and the growth of comfortable brick-built towns. By the time of Percy's birth it had reached a sumptuous maturity; the elms were in full sail, the towns were mellow.

In 1913 it was possible for an Englishman to pass his entire life unaware of the state, beyond the policeman and the postman. He could travel wherever he wanted without a passport, or buy and sell in any country in the world. For the fifty or so people who served or depended on Horwood House, however, the world was a more confined place. There was a railway station a half a mile from the house at Swanbourne, on the Oxford-Bletchley branch of the London &

North Western Railway, by which London could be reached fifty-one miles away. But that was a remote and different world. Even the county town of Aylesbury was far enough away to make a visit a very long day trip. Everything that the working community of Horwood House wanted of a town was to be found at Winslow, two and a half miles away and easily accessible even on foot.

Yet there were changes in the air, changes of which the very existence of the brand new Horwood House was a symptom. The traditional, long-established landowners, although not seriously bothered by death duties and taxation until after the First World War, had in numerous spectacular instances succumbed to agricultural depression, compounding generations of improvidence and slack management, gone under and sold up, bringing a vast acreage on to the market at relatively low prices. The extinction of the dukes of Buckingham and Chandos, of Stowe, had changed the social appearance of Buckinghamshire during the childhood of Percy's parents. The new grandees were people of a different and unknown sort. Their power and position rested on unprecedented wealth derived from trade or banking, rather than the fruits of public office and generations of marriages with heiresses. They were people, furthermore, who could often remember life over the shop and sometimes actual poverty; who now used their wealth with caution and managed it in a business-like way. By the turn of the century, five members of the Rothschild family alone had bought estates and built houses in north Buckinghamshire. But there was room for the lesser rich with the same instincts and ambitions, among them Frederick Denny, whose fortune lay in pork and bacon.

Denny was one of the first generation of his family to enjoy the ease of inherited wealth; but he remained involved in the running of the family business, going once or twice a week from his house in Down Street, opposite Green Park, to its headquarters in Lambeth. Although brought up mainly in London, he listed his recreations in *Who's Who* as 'hunting, shooting and fishing', and when he married in 1888 it was into a county family. Maude Quilter was one of the large family of a Suffolk baronet of Bawdsey Manor, near the sea south-east of Woodbridge. Her brothers included Roger Quilter, the once celebrated and by no means forgotten composer of songs, mainly settings of poems, in which, according to his biographer, 'he sought to enchant rather than to edify . . . in a voice unmistakably English and in a tone of voice unmistakably his own'. It was with his own growing family in mind that Frederick Denny decided to acquire a house in the country.

At Horwood he bought an estate which formed a modest, self-sufficient relic of old Buckinghamshire, consisting of 482 acres, two farms, eleven cottages, parkland and woods and, in due time, a house and gardens. There had been a house on the site, a farmhouse that had been built over three centuries. It was known as Rectory House, its owner being Lay Rector of Little Horwood, responsible for collecting the tithes on behalf of the vicar, and the freeholder of the church of St Nicholas. This was a position which Denny acquired with the property; it made him, in effect, squire. Horwood was also in the heart of the Whaddon Chase country, so he could at last hunt from home.

The years before the First World War were the last great period for country house building, although already the most popular architects were those who, like Norman Shaw, specialized in somewhat scaled-down forms of the gentlemen's seats of earlier years, or, like Blow and Billerey, offered a complete, tasteful package of house, interior decoration and

3

gardens. Denny commissioned Detmar Blow to design his house. Blow, who was architect to the Grosvenor Estate, the massively enriching Mayfair acreage of the Duke of Westminster, contracted Cubitts, who had developed much of the Grosvenor Estate's Belgravia property seventy years before, to do the actual building. Denny's instructions to Blow and the interior designer Billerey were exact: he wanted a house that was reasonably imposing but compact enough to be comfortable, and a design that recalled some of the characteristics of the former Rectory House; above all, he wanted the house to look as if it had always been there, in a setting that had matured with it.

Blow and Billerey made imaginative use of their materials towards these ends. Small, old reddish-brown bricks were procured from Holland and, to complete the antique effect, laid in the Flemish bond. The roof tiles, too, were old and weathered; and while the Bath stone of the cornice, mullions and transoms was new, it could be expected to fade into harmony with the rest over a couple of seasons. Inside, the effect of age was partly achieved by the perfectly legitimate means of having the panelling painted – brown for the dining-room, apple-green for the drawing-room – and where natural wood was used it was unstained oak, sand-blasted and beeswaxed, awaiting only the attention of generations of housemaids to bring it to perfection. The principal rooms – drawing-room, dining-room, parlour – interconnected along the south side of the house, overlooking a short lawn to the ha-ha, with pasture and established trees beyond. Upstairs there were fourteen bedrooms and dressing-rooms and five bathrooms. The kitchens and nine-bedroomed servants' wing, built on a smaller scale and to a simpler design, ran from the east side of the house, and adjoined the thatched stableyard which housed the Denny's eight highly-prized hunters.

In 1912, surprisingly quickly, it was all finished. The house won the warm approval of *Country Life,* which published an article about it. The Dennys were very well pleased. The arched entrance lodge on the road to the village even gave an impression that the place might have been a fortified manor house. But the coat of arms cut in stone on the chimney-piece in the hall of the house was not Frederick Denny's (they were there merely for effect), and the stately avenue of limes along the quarter mile between the lodge and the forecourt was yet to be planted. The house was beautiful but clinical; it had not seen a birth or a death nor even a quarrel. Outside, even Blow and Billerey could not produce an instant garden. Such things may be almost commonplace in California today but they were unknown, and would probably have been repugnant to, Edwardian Buckinghamshire. Care had been taken to pre-serve the fine trees, among them a cedar of Lebanon, weeping chestnut and perfectly-shaped oak, in what had been the gardens of Rectory House, and a six-roomed cottage had been built for the head gardener, standing at what was envisaged as the traditional point where pleasure and kitchen gardens met. Thereafter it was up to the owners, and their head gardener, to achieve what they could in the service of carefully nurtured nature.

Frederick Denny's head gardener, Harry Thrower, came originally from his wife's family's estate, Bawdsey Manor, in Suffolk. The name Thrower (meaning someone who twists the fibre – properly wool – into thread or yarn) is peculiar to East Anglia where it was adopted by people in parts of the weaving industry. Harry was born in 1882. In due time he married Beatrice Dunnett, of a family from Walberswick,

5

further up the Suffolk coast, who were fishermen with a certain sideline in smuggling. Harry trained in the fairly bleak horticultural conditions of Bawdsey and then proceeded as a journeyman-gardener to King's Waldenbury in Hertford-shire, where he later became a foreman. The estate adjoined that of the Earl and Countess of Strathmore at St Paul's Waldenbury, where the future Queen Elizabeth was then growing up surrounded by a celebrated garden.

Before Harry Thrower's appointment to Horwood, he and Beatrice had one son, who was named after his father. Their second son, Percy John, was the first child to be born at the new Horwood. Between 1913 and 1920 their family grew to include two girls, Maude and Joan, and a third son, Maurice.

By becoming head gardener while still in his twenties, Harry Thrower had risen as far as it was then possible for a professional gardener in private service to go. His position was not unenviable. Gardens should be started when one is young, and he was young enough. The land in his charge, which Percy first remembered as just woodland and rough pasture, eventually consisted of six highly cultivated acres. He was the master of sixteen men, some of them highly skilled in their various specialities. His pay of £2 a week, with a house, free vegetables, housing, heating and miscellaneous perks, may have been no better than the butler's but in the establishment's pecking order his place was rather higher.

A good head gardener was a valued member of a country house, with a degree of power in upholding the owner's reputation and self-esteem. Victorian plutocrats, and their successors into the present century for as long as the money lasted, were a competitive breed. On the turf or on their yachts, they were there not only to be seen but to be seen to win. At home the battleground was the dining-table and what was on it, whether for consumption or display. At Horwood, Harry Thrower had to keep to the fashionable target date of Queen Mary's birthday, 26 May, for having peaches ready to eat. Mrs Denny took particular pleasure in the finer variations of colour and whenever she and her husband returned from a visit to a house where something exotic or out of season had been on show, questions would be asked about doing the same at Horwood. The Dennys, however, generally deferred to Harry in his domain: there was a convention of near equality, based on a shared interest, between master and head gardener.

Percy could remember only one occasion when Mr Denny actually overruled his father. This was when the hunt was close to Horwood House and the hounds were clearly going to chase the fox into the kitchen garden. Percy and his family enjoyed the spectacle of hunting and presumed the fox must enjoy it, but they also had to live with the terrible havoc that hounds could wreak in gardens. On this occasion Harry shut the garden gates against them. Denny did not order Harry to reopen the gates; he dismounted and did so himself. The damage, though not irreparable, ruined weeks of work in the crowded garden year.

The garden into which Percy Thrower was born and where he grew up was a 365-day-a-year way of life. The Throwers' house adjoined the kitchen garden, as was customary for a head gardener's house. The slightly rectangular two acres of kitchen garden were enclosed by brick walls ten feet high which were aligned to provide the maximum possible space for the plants, especially the fruits, in their preferred aspects. Fruit trees covered most of the walls: apples and pears, grown as espaliers, and morello cherries on the north; dessert cherries on the east; more apples and pears on the west; and peaches and nectarines fan-trained on the warm south-facing wall. The south and north borders were given to early and late vegetable crops respectively, with the maincrops in four beds in the main body of the garden. The lean-to glasshouses, heated by water pipes fed by an anthracite-fired boiler, and with all-metal frames, were of an advanced design for their time but suffered dreadfully from condensation. Despite such problems, the climates in the houses had to be controlled to suit the many purposes they served, whether for melons and cucumbers, carnations, or propagating.

The potting-shed doubled as Harry Thrower's office. Unlike many head gardeners he was not just a manager or overseer but also worked with his men and as far as practicable reserved certain jobs, such as pruning the fruit trees, to himself. His formal study of horticulture may have been confined to reading the seed catalogues, but his gardening methods were founded on highly intelligent experience, frequently enlivened by instinct. He could tell by the air on a March morning whether or not it was the day to start sowing and would try the soil only to confirm what he had already decided.

The image of the vegetable garden is not a lovely one. 'Who,' asked Jane Austen, 'can endure a cabbage bed in October?' A kitchen garden such as Horwood's, however, was designed to look pleasing as well as to be productive. Besides the vegetables there were flowers for cutting for decorating the house and an abundance of rambling roses of old, highly-scented varieties. At its centre there was a round pond, planted with water-lilies, and a fountain to provide a soothing background of running water. The riotous abundance of it all was given an air of formality by the box edges of the main plots, although their cover was paradise for slugs and snails and their clipping, next to scarifying the lawns or weeding the paved paths, the meanest and most back-breaking job in the garden. Surveyed from the potting-shed the kitchen garden had something of the appearance, though hardly the contents, of a garden in a medieval palace or monastery. Like the custodian of one of the latter, Harry Thrower had the beehives and their sublimely ordered life in his care.

There was a minor threat to all this order when Percy, his siblings and their friends were old enough to be about the place. Although he was only the second son, Percy (known as John at home because the younger children could not get their tongues round Percy) was from quite early on the strongest personality in the group. In all but the very earliest family photographs it is Percy's level gaze that dominates. His elder brother Harry was essentially a quieter and more restrained type. Percy's natural tendencies were enhanced by the exist-ence of two younger sisters and a brother, to whom he was variously a protector and a hero. There was also a streak of exceptional tenacity in Percy. Charles Heady, a lifelong friend from these years, recalls that his father would point to him as an example and say that he could properly have been named 'Perseverance' rather than Percy.

But there was ample work for idle hands in the garden. What Harry's men said about the children would probably be unprintable. They would turn out, for example, at the end of the long day to prepare to go home and find their jackets neatly hung up but turned inside out with the sleeves tied together. Jimmy Barford, the elderly wood and coal man who walked to work from Great Horwood five miles away with a back pack in which to take away a modest supply of firewood, would heave the pack on to his back in the evenings and, having all but collapsed under the weight, find that the wood had been replaced with bricks. Some of their pranks would have worked on the silent screen. Walking along outside the servants' wing one evening, juggling some windfalls with his friend Charles Heady, Percy lobbed a rotten apple through an open bathroom window on the first floor and scuttled off pursued by an outraged shriek from within. Some of their amusements were frankly rather unpleasant, like firing at the men with an airgun from a range that would be sure to sting. The men sometimes got their own back, on one occasion by lacing some of the home-made wine, which Percy's mother made from just about everything, with paraffin, so that when the boys took an illicit draught they were copiously sick.

Percy's father's disciplinary methods were simple, direct and unanswerably effective in the short term, even though dozens more thrashings were threatened than actually given. If he spotted trouble from a distance he would make for the scene bawling 'Come here! You little buggers!', and, if he was close enough, throw his cap at them. He was highly skilled with this weapon. Even so, as often as not it ended up in a pond or the branches of a tree, leaving Harry in an even greater rage. Although still quite a young man when Percy was in his early boyhood, Harry Thrower had already developed the slightly bent figure and slow but highly efficient manner of moving that is one of the hallmarks of a real gardener. Another way to spot a gardener is by his hands which, although coarsened by the nature of the work, are strong but sensitive, and delicate in their movements.

When the children ventured into the pleasure garden they had to behave themselves. They were told to keep out of it altogether when the Dennys were at home. If they did encounter them they were scrupulously polite, in the certain

10

knowledge that they would be shown kindness and consideration in return. Percy always retained a sense of rank. When he had become a national figure and found himself in conversation with a ducal enthusiast or the like he would observe the correct forms of address without embarrassment and with more relish than deference.

The Thrower children were most likely to talk to the Dennys on Sunday mornings. At St Nicholas's Church in Little Horwood Percy sang in the choir, with an unusually vivid medieval wall painting of the Seven Deadly Sins on one side and the Ten Commandments stamped on burnished brass on the other. The Dennys sat in their special pew, making a mental note of who from their staff was present and who was not. After church some of the garden men hurried back to wash and brush the already immaculate carnation house floor, ready for the Dennys' ritual Sunday morning inspection and selection of buttonholes.

On his tombstone in Little Horwood churchyard, Harry Thrower is remembered as 'Highly valued friend and head gardener for many years to Mr and Mrs Denny of Horwood House'. The real memorial to this friendship was the garden. Apart from undertakings such as the planting of the avenue of limes from the lodge to the house, most of the creative gardening was done to the east and south of the house. The end of the house away from the servants' wing looked across the site of the former Rectory House, on which an *étang* was made. An *étang* was a piece of ornamental water of natural origin, first made an art at Fontainebleau in the sixteenth century. The one at Horwood was fed by a spring that had served Rectory House. It was enclosed by a yew hedge, planted with some simple topiary in mind, and had a fine backdrop in the old trees of the Rectory House garden. As well

11

as the inevitable water-lilies there were, most unusually for that time, standard fuchsias in pots placed around the edges.

Within relatively modest limits, the garden contained many contrasts and cleverly achieved great variety; between the artfully wild and the happily regimented, between the formal and the informal. South of the *étang* a flight of steps led down to the true garden, beginning with a flagged path between deep herbaceous borders towards a mysterious-looking wood. Half way to the wood there was a walled garden with a formal pond in the middle, planted with water-lilies but with enough of the surface left clear to allow reflections of the nearby elms and sometimes even of clouds passing overhead. The water supply to the pond was concealed by a *Cotoneaster horizontalis*, a fine example of Harry's imaginative and highly effective use of an often rather nasty-looking shrub.

Beyond was ground which was being brought into cultivation. Plantations of silver birches faced brave attempts to establish bold groups of rhododendrons. The rhododendrons never thrived on the neutral-to-limey soil – even though the site was exhaustively prepared to suit them. In those days before chemical supplements with which to treat the soil regularly it soon reverted to its original composition.

There were few such problems in the bog garden, which was one of Harry Thrower's proudest creations. It was based on a stream which had been enlarged and diverted to form a small, branching lake. The making of it had been one of the projects on which Percy and his friends worked during their school holidays. In its formative days the ground in the garden was so boggy that planks had to be laid across the mire to take wheelbarrows. There was plenty of scope for playing about, and Percy and the others spent as much time making

12

mud balls to try and throw through the D-handles of their spades as on digging and damming. Many of the plants – senecio, saxifrage, spiraea – chose themselves. Harry was particularly fond of primulas which he established in the bog garden in many varieties planned to flower over a very long season. One of the most satisfying jobs which Percy recalled from his early years was of cutting off the seed pods of the primulas at the end of their season and scattering them over further marshy areas of the woodland.

Another of Harry's enthusiasms was for *Meconopsis baileyi* (blue poppy-like flowers), of which he developed a large stock. These and certain varieties of primula were a prey to pirates from seed merchants and when the gardens were open to the public at Whitsun each year Percy and Ken White, one of his schoolfriends, were instructed to keep a particular eye open for such people. Harry also excelled with begonias and cyclamen, and with calceolarias, for which he was awarded a Banksian medal, the Royal Horticultural Society's oldest award, given for exhibits of flowers and ornamental plants, at Chelsea and the Society's other shows where he and his fellow head gardeners regularly met.

Harry Thrower's gardening was generally informed by the country, soil and climate of Horwood; but his friends included head gardeners elsewhere such as Mentmore, one of the nearby Rothschild houses, whose owners were more demanding than the Dennys in their taste for the exotic. When the Dennys went away they often brought home seeds or cuttings of unfamiliar plants for Harry to work on. Their visits to the Earl and Countess of Stair at Castle Kennedy in Galloway were especially productive. The Stairs' garden, on acid soil in the exceptionally mild climate of south-west Scotland, contained much that satisfied Mrs Denny's fondness for

13

strong colours. It was from there, for example, that the idea came for planting large groups of rhododendrons and azaleas; and with the idea came many of the plants with which Harry fought a losing battle at Horwood over the years. The giant Himalayan lily (*Cardiocrinum giganteum*) was another introduction from Castle Kennedy, after Harry had been there on holiday himself, and one that found Horwood more comfortable. This enormous lily, growing up to eight feet tall, could be considered the floral equivalent of the giant prize-winning marrow. Some of the bulbs that Harry gave Percy to plant in the bog garden were the size of footballs. It was a couple of years before they produced any flowers and there would be a similar interlude before they flowered again. Harry was evidently very taken by them; the bulbils were collected, nurtured, replanted and eventually filled a complete border in the kitchen garden.

In Percy's early experience of gardening there was more observation than practice. Like the great apple breeder Thomas Rivers, before him, he began to learn about apples by watching and tasting in a well-stocked orchard. Up to the First World War the best fruit-tree growers offered around 500 varieties of apple alone. Of these a selection of 200 had been made for the Horwood orchard. They had been chosen with the longest possible season in mind, so that for all but a few midsummer weeks a stock was always available in fair condition. The way to school lay through the orchard and Percy used his discerning eye to supplement his lunch with a few borrowed apples.

Little Horwood Church of England School seldom had more than forty pupils. It stood behind the church, and was reached by a path across the boundary of the churchyard and past a cottage where a retired schoolmistress lived with her parrot, which was given to occasional outbursts of random parts of the tables, picked-up from years of hearing the children practise them. During Percy's time the school was in the charge of a husband and wife named Davies. Their job cannot have been particularly encouraging. While their pupils were no more unwilling, and on the whole neither more nor less gifted or backward, than any others, the Davieses worked in the knowledge that at the age of fourteen virtually all of them would leave school and go to work on the farms or for the houses from which they came. 'PT', as Mr Davies called Percy, was restive for the garden from the first. He was not the only one with this tendency and the Davieses made the most of it educationally by having the children cultivate small plots behind the school building. When judgement was pronounced upon them Percy's garden was invariably top. He also helped the Davieses with their own garden, and continued to work for his father on Saturdays and during the school holidays.

Percy always claimed that on the academic side he had been very average at school. Yet when in 1927 Mr Davies came to press for one or two of his more promising pupils to be allowed to go on to the Royal Latin School in Buckingham, which with effort and a bit of luck could lead to anything, Percy was one of his more hopeful prospects of the year. The idea was proposed to ears that were not so much deaf as closed to the idea of education beyond the essential. And so Percy left school and went properly to work; his first job, like those of his brothers and sisters, was provided by Horwood House. The break meant that in later years when ambition had taken hold of him and he began to study for horticultural qualifications Percy had to work doubly hard to improve his basic learning skills. But for the time being he had all that he needed. He seems to have been born with a gift for organizing other people and in adolescence was already a good enough communicator to make a memorable, if unconventional, Sunday School teacher. At home he had learnt how to behave with decorum towards people of widely different backgrounds. Above all he had absorbed some of the unteachable mysteries of the garden by living in one. He had developed an ambition to achieve excellence in the garden and, in due time, to become a head gardener like his father.

Whether or not the gardens or Horwood House actually needed another pot-and-crock boy in the spring of 1927 was not a consideration that entered the heads of either Harry Thrower or the Dennys. To the Dennys the provision of a job for an able and very willing boy of Percy's particular background was a question of *noblesse oblige*. The pay and conditions were those that would have been offered in the open market; one shilling for an eleven-hour, 6.30–5.30 day, with half an hour allowed for breakfast at 8.00, an hour for dinner at 12.30, and a 1.30 finish on Saturdays. Work began and finished at 6.30 and 5.30; preparation and clearing-up, the cleaning, oiling and stacking of tools and equipment, had to be done outside these hours, although there were agreed rates of pay for real overtime.

Fully kitted-out in a blue apron and leaden-heavy boots, Percy was inspected by his mother and seen off the few yards to the potting-shed to report ready for work to his father. His first tasks, performed under the eye of one of the boys who was barely his senior, were simple glasshouse chores such as sweeping the floor and clinkering the boiler, which he had been spared in the days when he was really about the garden to play; but he was soon allowed to try more gardenly skills such as pricking out and potting on. Harry Thrower was ubiquitous with advice, encouragement and warnings. He was still somewhat irascible, and while the threats of a thrashing had been replaced by equally regular threats of the sack, the flying cap was still in use as a weapon and in the confines of the glasshouse, perhaps mercifully, more often than not hit its intended target.

The glasshouses were no place for the heavy-handed; nor was any casual behaviour or sloppy work tolerated in them. Apart from the glass itself, much that was grown in the houses was delicate and expensive to rear. The melons, for example, hanging from the roof each in its own net cradle, or the cucumbers, protected and kept straight by highly vulnerable long tubes of glass, or the grapes, whether still on the vine or stored and kept fresh by the bunch in half-reclining bottles with water made sweet by the addition of charcoal. The beginners had a role in controlling the climate of the glasshouses. To them fell the task of patrolling the houses on hot days with a water-filled syringe, spraying the floors and the plants in an attempt to keep the humidity up. Once the novelty had worn off it was a job of soul-destroying tedium to anybody with less imagination than a poet. The syringes were put to more dramatic use in the forcing processes. Peach trees, for example, were syringed twice a day in mid-winter with slightly warmed water to get the sap running and at length brought into blossom months ahead of their time and almost before one's eyes.

Outside, the kitchen garden was run on the classic principles of rotation, derived from the studies of plant nutrition by the early-nineteenth-century chemist Sir Humphry Davy. Brassicas (cabbage, broccoli, Brussels sprouts and so on), known as 'deteriorators' because they were such greedy feeders, would be grown on recently manured ground which had been previously rested. They would be followed by root crops (potatoes, carrots, onions and the like) known as 'preparers'. Then would come a sowing of green 'surface' crops (beans, peas, lettuce and other salads). Thereafter the ground would be rested for some time, perhaps as a strawberry bed, before a new cycle was begun on it.

In those days before branded fertilizers and composts gardeners had to prepare their own for different purposes and all had their tried and preferred recipes. There was at least an abundance of farmyard manure. It could be used for climatic as well as nutritional purposes: cauliflowers, for example, could be planted on a slight hotbed of manure as early as February. A healthy horse produces about thirty tons of dung a year, and so with the Dennys' eight hunters and many lesser beasts about the place there was a bottomless supply. Cow dung, which was cooler than horse's because of the cow's diet of grass and water, was favoured for fruit trees, and was equally readily available at Horwood. But sheep dung, which was particularly valued for its high content of phosphates and nitrogen, was rather thinner on the ground. Bone-meal was used less in those days as a soil conditioner than as a fertilizer, which would nurture vegetables that were both better looking and better suited to human nutrition. Bone-crushing machines were invented in the early nineteenth century and the English greed for bones raised passions amongst agricultural chemists.

Harry Thrower was a regular and respected enough customer of the seed merchants to be sent samples of new varieties for trial. He also kept well abreast of new developments in the vegetables he grew for supplies to the house. Some of the varieties of common vegetable introduced then are still favourites today. Other vegetables grown are very seldom encountered now, partly because they have been superseded or because they were sometimes difficult to prepare for the table and not at all agreeable to look at when they got there. The long, black roots of scorzonera (viper's grass), for example, might be tender and juicy enough to eat when thoroughly boiled but they remained defiantly black; or the magnificent, celery-like cardoon, which grew up to seven feet high, after hacking and whittling yielded only enough to play a modest role in a large stew.

Helping to carry the day's supply of vegetables up to the house had been part of Percy's way of life from childhood. Now, he and some of the other garden men took off their boots twice a week and went into the house, on Friday mornings to prepare the flower arrangements ready for the Dennys' return from London, and then on Tuesday mornings to clear up after they had gone away again. This notion of the weekend, deplored and despised by the aristocracy, was nonetheless highly agreeable to those with a limited amount of work to do and very convenient to people with a house as close to London as Horwood. Even the railway delivered the Dennys almost to their front door; but increasingly in the twenties they travelled by road, when three chauffeurs and several motors joined the traditional community in the stableyard.

Flower arranging was a man's job in those days, as it remains in a diminishing number of great houses. Their arrangements were practical and efficient rather than artistic, based on the very sound principle that, though out of their element, suitably accommodated flowers would presently arrange themselves. It awaited a more self-conscious age and the missionary attitudes of Constance Spry and Julia Clements, among others, to make an art of flower

19

arrangement – an art in which Percy's eldest daughter Margaret was to shine.

Percy's first job in the house on a Friday morning was a more conventionally manly one. Special boxes were brought in filled with straw and placed in various unseen spots around the dining-room for the purpose of absorbing the reek of cigars which would otherwise linger after dinner overnight. Thereafter they proceeded to the flower arrangements throughout the house, including Mrs Denny's boudoir up-stairs where Percy and his friend Ken White enlisted the help of the housemaids to complete an enjoyable morning. On weekday afternoons in summer the housemaids would be lured out to play cricket on the lawn between the house and the ha-ha. Provided no damage was done and everything returned to order after the game, nobody seemed to mind.

These were the girls whom Percy and his friends used to 'escort' to dances in Little and Great Horwood, Swanbourne and Mursley on Saturday nights. They could hardly go further afield because they were obliged to go on foot and, a little later, by the comparative luxury of a bicycle. Percy's bicycle was chosen from a catalogue and bought on hire purchase of fifty shillings at two shillings and sixpence a week. His father was unaware of how Percy had come by the bicycle until, to his mortification, the spokes of the front wheel were damaged by a cricket ball while the bicycle lay in the long grass by the boundary. Harry cleared the outstand-ing hire purchase debt from his own pocket and gave Percy a lifetime's warning against borrowing money. The bicycle could, just about, carry a girl as a passenger to and from a dance; but what Percy yearned for, for this and other excur-sions, was a motor bike, the pillion of which would certainly attract the bolder girls.

Percy himself was bold enough by comparison with the generally shy and quaintly high-minded youths of Little Horwood. He had begun to take an interest in his appearance quite soon after he left school. By the age of sixteen or seventeen his then abundant fair hair was well groomed and his strong, watchful blue eyes could on occasions be tellingly still. When they went off to a dance without escorts Percy invariably ended up with the best girl in the room, even though he would go outside from time to time to take a fortifying swig from a bottle of British port purchased on the way at 'The Crown' in Little Horwood for three shillings and sixpence. Similarly, when a semi-professional company performed the melodrama *Murder at the Red Barn* in the village hall at Great Horwood, it was Percy who made the acquaintance of the leading lady.

All this social life needed money beyond his basic wages in the garden. Apart from overtime there was money to be made in the garden from catching pests and predators. Moles, for example, commanded sixpence each and at some seasons there were so many that Percy's takings from them was sometimes greater than his week's wage. Then there were rabbits, preferably netted for in that condition they were better for cooking or could be sold for a good price. Mrs Thrower's rabbit pie was one of the rather frequent occasions that caused Harry to call for a bottle of British port from 'The Crown'. Other potations were drawn from Mrs Thrower's huge supplies of home-made wines: dandelion, cowslip, celery, wheat, raisin, elderberry, potato and elderflower (among others), most of them higher in alcohol than anything normally encountered by the Customs and Excise men, all kept for a year or so in five-gallon casks, then bottled ready for use. Some, such as elderberry, were sometimes used when the children were ill or had colds. But most were kept for the evenings when one or other of the Throwers' peers in the household would invariably call, to talk, perhaps to play cards, or just to sit together in silence in the way that very old friends can do without embarrassment. Once in bed Harry, in particular, slept deeply, not just the sleep of one who spent his days at work in the open air but of one who had spent a very relaxing evening.

Harry's hands, however, remained steady and his eyes clear. He was an excellent shot, and first allowed Percy to try his hand with a double-barrelled shotgun when he was about twelve, rabbits taking the place of the unfortunate garden men he had persecuted with his airgun. Shooting was to become the only recreation to which he admitted in later life, and although never a first-class shot he was still getting better on his last day out with a gun in the early winter of 1987–88, a matter of months before his death.

Shooting ran hunting a close second in Mr Denny's recreations and he was generous to the staff with pheasants and lesser game birds when they were in season and with humbler fare like pigeons at other times. The smallest birds could also be the greatest delicacies. Blackbirds, caught by accident and killed in the fruit cages, made a superb meal when quickly roasted. Rooks, on the other hand, the Throwers could not abide. Rook pie was a minor delicacy to the upper classes (albeit one which seemed to peak in popularity when nothing else was in season to be shot at). Denny was as generous with rooks as all his other bags and the Throwers had to dispose of them without causing him offence. This was not always easy to do discreetly, for among their many endearing characteristics rooks are inclined to come down from the elms and stand around in solemn groups to mourn their departed.

By his eighteenth year Percy had certain responsible jobs at Horwood but no formal position, nor any prospect of one. Before he could be considered for any job that would fulfil his ambition of becoming a head gardener, he had the lesser grades of improver, journeyman and foreman to work through. His recognized responsibilities of looking after the boilers that heated the glasshouses and bicycling into Lloyds Bank in Winslow on Fridays to collect the wages, were clearly not enough to occupy one of his energy, skill and ambition. Besides, there was perhaps some doubt whether he would ever grow up in the circumstances of Horwood and learn to take life and his work entirely seriously.

It would be against every rule that he should ever succeed his father at Horwood. Besides, Harry Thrower was not only still not fifty years old, but his empire was shrinking alarmingly, along with the garden staffs at all private estates, as the depression of the 1930s took hold. Harry's workforce of sixteen was to shrink to seven by 1931. His friends, the head gardeners at Mentmore, Tring, Luton Hoo and elsewhere reported the same decline, with the younger, unmarried men always the first to be laid off. Within the decade – within one generation – Horwood House would be sold and turned to the first of a succession of institutional uses. Within the decade also, as things turned out, Harry Thrower would be dead at the age of fifty-seven.

There was the still relatively prosperous world of municipal and civic gardening for Percy to go to but nobody at Horwood knew much about it in 1930. Mrs Denny's connections in the horticultural world did not come up with any firm offers, either.

The only private gardens that for the time being were not cutting back were the gardens of the various royal houses.

The largest and grandest royal gardening establishment was at Windsor. The Horwood people knew a little about Windsor; the owners of the former Rectory House had supplied Queen Victoria with a particular type of cheese. Harry Thrower was also acquainted with the head gardener at Windsor, Charles Cook, with whom he had occasionally judged at flower and horticultural shows. A letter was sent and an interview arranged; Percy was taken on at Windsor as an improver. His pay would be £1 a week, although with the loss of the other earnings to which he had become accustomed the move would probably lead to a drop in income. Mrs Denny supplied a fulsome 'character'; the vicar, Mr Dunham, testified to Percy's moral probity. Mr Denny, swollen with vicarious pride, supplied his car and his chauffeur to drive Percy to Windsor. And so he swept out of Horwood in unprecedented style and a cloud of dust, and the rooks settled and cawed reassuringly to those who were left behind.

2

Windsor

At the time he went to Windsor in 1931 Percy had seldom slept away from Horwood House. Family holidays had been worked around visits to towns where Harry Thrower had been judging at horticultural shows. Such was the lot of head gardeners' children. Percy's mother had also taken him away occasionally on a few days' visit to his Dunnett grandparents at the little fishing village of Walberswick on the Suffolk coast. The way of life of the fishermen was by nature less ordered and repetitive than the unchanging daily routine Percy knew at Horwood. There was a different flavour to the evenings also when, after Percy was in bed, the house would be curiously quiet and shut up while his grandfather and his cronies enjoyed some of their contraband in a darkened back room. One of the more familiar pleasures of these rare holidays was going duck shooting on the marshes with his grandfather. His grandfather kept a black Labrador, a working gun dog like Mr Denny's, and it became one of Percy's lesser ambitions to have one of his own.

It was at Walberswick that he came closest to the First World War, on trips into the surrounding country and up and down the coast where shelling by German warships had left huge craters in the ground. With the keen air and the landscape at places sliding almost imperceptibly into the North Sea, it was all quite remote from Horwood.

On the other hand there was much about Windsor and the surrounding area that was essentially familiar to Percy. As he travelled south from Horwood the elm-dotted, undramatic landscape continued. There were many fine eighteenth-century buildings in Wendover, Amersham, Beaconsfield and Slough, that would have looked equally at home in Winslow. The surprises were all at the very end of the journey. The workman-like houses of Eton, huddled around the College; the River Thames, at this point still narrow but already sluggish; a vertiginous street in the permanent shadow of Windsor Castle; and then his destination, a prospect revealed as suddenly as a theatrical set when the curtain rises, the huge sweep of the Home Park with, perhaps, a flash in the middle distance from the sun on the roofs of the glasshouses in the Royal Gardens.

The gardening instinct runs very deep in the British royal family, although it was not until well into the nineteenth century that Windsor came to be to any extent the centre of its gardening activity. The Great Park and the Home Park at Windsor are the 5,000-acre remnant of what was once a vast tract of country reserved for hunting, which extended from Reading to Chertsey and from Guildford well into Buckinghamshire. There were tiny gardens within the Castle precincts, exquisite refuges from the crush of court life. Some of these survive, besides more conspicuous additions such as the grand parterre on the East Terrace. But in the seventeenth and eighteenth centuries royal gardeners were busier else-where. Charles I began the labyrinthine waterworks at Hampton Court which were to make practicable the gardens laid out by George London and Henry Wise for their patrons William and Mary, and Queen Anne. Fifty years later King George II and the son he detested, Frederick, Prince of Wales, lived on the adjacent estates of Richmond Gardens and Kew House. Partly to ease the unpleasantness of this propinquity, they each laid out highly ambitious grounds, from which evolved the Royal Botanic Gardens.

At Windsor, Charles II had begun the taming of the hunting forest by having the three-mile elm avenue known as the Long Walk planted, running south from the Castle. The later Hanoverians penetrated further into the Park, especially a Duke of Cumberland (the 'butcher' of Culloden), who had the lake at Virginia Water made. At the outer end of the Long Walk the surviving children of George III erected a huge equestrian bronze (known, perversely, as the 'Copper Horse') to his memory which, because of its position, commands this part of the Berkshire landscape more than the Castle itself.

The concentration of royal gardening activity in the south-eastern quarter of the Home Park, near the Castle and beside the Long Walk, began when Queen Charlotte, wife of George III, retired to Frogmore House. Queen Charlotte was a knowl-edgeable enthusiast for apples (the dish Apple Charlotte is said to have been named after her), who had several of the rooms of the house painted to designs dominated by garlands of flowers, and the grounds laid out in the picturesque style by Sir Uvedale Price, the landscape architect who rejected the principles of Capability Brown and Humphrey Repton in favour of a manner which he perceived to be closer to the ideals displayed in the paintings of Poussin or Claude.

There was no place for the picturesque when Prince Albert got to work on the area of the Home Park next to Frogmore House sixty years later. The Prince was the most methodical of all royal gardeners. He was well abreast of all new tastes and techniques, and would be there to supervise and lend a hand in the more important works himself. His influence was at its most free and expansive in the gardens he designed for the new Osborne House on the Isle of Wight, where he was responsible for planting cherry laurel (*Prunus laurocerasus*), thus, it has been said, ensuring 'the popularity of the unhappiest features of nineteenth century gardening'.

At Windsor the Prince built a Dairy, decorated with Minton tiles, a Home Farm and an Aviary, all according to the most exacting modern standards of their day. He was in pursuit of the advance of scientific gardening at his very last public appearance in 1861, when he opened the Royal Horticultural Society's garden at Kensington on a site near the museums and institutes of his own foundation, in an 'attempt to reunite the science and art of gardening to the sister arts of architecture, sculpture and painting'.

The buildings of the fruit and flower gardens – the Royal Gardens in which Percy went to work – were mainly erected during the reign of Edward VII. At the centre of them was a house far more immediately imposing to Percy than any of the nearby grace-and-favour houses and follies-cum-lodges, let alone Windsor Castle itself. This was the substantial neo-Tudor house where the head gardener, Charles Cook, a man of powerful build and presence, lived with his family. In many ways they were more remote than the Dennys at Horwood.

Most of the head gardeners at Windsor have been of Scottish origin. Gardening may be of all the arts that which is quintessentially English but many of its most influential practitioners have not been strictly speaking English themselves. At the present time the keepers of some of the most celebrated English gardens are in fact of central European origin. William Robinson, one of the most followed practical gardeners of all time, who made the garden at Gravetye Manor in Sussex, was Irish. So also was Charles Cook, whose father was head gardener at Kilshayne and a begetter of notable gardeners.

Charles's brothers included Tom Cook, head gardener at Sandringham, Harry, head gardener at Reading University, and Sam, head gardener to the Cadbury family. In their contrasted ways these were three of the top jobs in British gardening and Charles's own position at Windsor was arguably the very top. On his way to Windsor Charles had worked for the Duke of Buccleuch at Dalkeith, near Edinburgh, and then for the Earl of Derby at Knowsley, near Liverpool. Until the First World War both these noblemen were considerably richer than King George V, but the head gardenership at Windsor was the position that anyone in the field would aspire to.

When Percy arrived there in 1931 the Royal Gardens employed sixty men, with up to twenty young improvers like himself in the bothy (where the labourers were lodged). According to the contractors, the glasshouses at Windsor were probably the largest private range in the world. There were fourteen Vineries, eight Peach Houses, three Fig Houses, two Palm Houses, six Orchid Houses, two Show Malmaison (a huge, highly-scented French carnation, now quite out of fashion) Houses, two Carnation Houses, two Flowering Show Houses, a Tropical House, a Laelia (orchid) House, two Propagating Houses, a number of Stove Houses, two Cypripedium (orchid) Houses, two Dendrobium (orchid) Houses, a Begonia House, two Cyclamen Houses, two Geranium Houses, three Azalea Houses, two Amaryllis Houses, a Fernery, four Cucumber Houses, four Melon Houses, two Tomato Houses, two Eucharis Houses, two Imantophyllum (cliria) Houses, two Pelargonium Houses, a Rose House and two connecting plant corridors. The houses needed 156,000 superficial feet of glass and the heating pipes totalled eleven miles.

29

Charles Cook could see most of all this from his house and from his office or numerous comfortable resting points around the gardens. Where Harry Thrower had planned and organized from the potting-shed, Cook worked from a well-furnished room with gothic windows. His erect bearing said everything about his position, although it was further underlined by his striped trousers and black jacket, a bowler hat or something taller for great occasions. Like royalty, who will never give an order and seldom express an opinion directly, so Cook worked through instructions given to his foremen and passed on for action. He would strut around the gardens looking sharply to left and right but, being a true aristocrat in his domain, would never dream of looking behind. This did not mean that anyone could relax over their work as soon as he had passed; as newcomers quickly discovered, he made a practice of retracing his steps at unpredictable intervals.

Apart from his presence, there was a certain grandeur in Cook's way of life. The head gardener's house had special rooms, most notably the Tea Room, set aside for the use George V and Queen Mary when they came down to the gardens. This could happen at any time when the Court was at Windsor, but particularly during regular summer festivals such as Ascot Week. The table in the Tea Room was decorated with, of all things, china pots with china roses in them. Here also were kept the innumerable silver spades and other garden tools that had been used and presented at ceremonial tree-plantings. Queen Mary was notorious for poking around antique shops, even very humble ones. It was an interest she had in common with Mrs Cook, and made conversation slightly less awkward.

In these circumstances it was not surprising that the Cooks may have been modestly ambitious for their children, and, in particular, for their two just nubile daughters, Constance and Mabel. The gardens were almost exclusively a man's world. Most of the men were married, apart from the twenty or so bothy boys who, by definition, were not. If any of them had thought fit to marry they would have been obliged to leave and try to find work at a level where married accommodation was available. In the eyes of the Cooks the bothy boys were thunderously ineligible, however wholesome and respectable they might be. The first instruction Percy could remember being given at Windsor was: 'Keep your eyes off the head gardener's daughters.'

A place in a bothy in a great garden – any great garden, let alone that at Windsor – was a rare privilege. They were lodgings where the trainee gardeners lived in common and to a large extent looked after themselves and one another. Some of them were almost uninhabitable, like the bothy at Ripley Castle in Yorkshire, which was literally in the dungeons. Getting a place in a good bothy could be haphazard. They were distinct communities, with their own cricket and football teams if they were large enough, and a place could sometimes be assured more by a good season on the cricket field than by years of proven diligence weeding the crazy paving. Most of the young men would not previously have lived away from home and would thus be far more clueless at rudimentary housekeeping than their contemporaries who had done five years in public schools. Geoffrey Hall, who became head gardener at Harewood House, near Leeds, recalled that during his bothy days at Warter Priory one of the lads was discovered trying to pluck a rabbit. The mysteries of cooking, washing-up, sewing, darning and bed-making were gradually unfolded by urgent need, by trial and error.

The bothy at Windsor was a fairly new E-shaped building

towards the north-east corner of the garden enclosure, away
from the town but a short walk from the gardeners' pub, the
'Lord Nelson' at Old Windsor. Although the men lived to a
large extent in common each had, unusually, a bedroom of his
own. The dining-room even had a wireless, from which the
legendary C. H. Middleton, the pre-war voice of gardening,
could be heard intoning after luncheon on Sundays: 'I hate to
be telling you to put manure on your rhubarb when you're
actually putting custard on yours.' A woman came in every
morning, apart from the weekends, to prepare the breakfast,
clear up, and get lunch ready. Otherwise they were left to
themselves. Meat, vegetables and milk were supplied free by
the establishment; butter, sugar, bread and jam had to be
bought, from the bothy caterer, to whom all accounts were
payable at the end of each week. With this expense, and
perhaps a couple of evenings a week in the 'Lord Nelson',
there was not often much left over from Percy's £1 (soon
raised to one guinea) pay each week. Dances in the town or
weekends at Horwood, which were in any case few and far
between because of the exacting work schedule at Windsor,
were matters for careful planning well in advance.

While they made no demands on the free time of the bothy
boys, the authorities at Windsor privately hoped that they
would give a certain amount of it to self-improvement and
working towards qualifications that would enable them to
develop their careers. The times were beginning to be felt
even at Windsor and, setting aside the unforeseeable and
drastic events of 1936, few if any of the bothy boys could
expect to spend the whole of their working lives at Windsor,
particularly if they wished to make much progress up the
professional hierarchy. The Royal Horticultural Society's non-
academic National Diploma in Horticulture had been estab-

lished in 1913 with just such people in mind and they were discreetly encouraged to work with an eye towards it.

Beyond the daily routine of the Royal Gardens there was much going on in the immediate area to inspire and instruct an intelligent apprentice. Windsor Great Park was ancient woodland, partly tamed and landscaped in the eighteenth century with a natural destiny to reach its prime around the middle of the present century. All this lay on the very doorstep of the Royal Gardens, within sight of Percy's bedroom window. Yet for all its abundance there was not within the confines of the Great Park a single pleasure garden; the pleasures for which the Park had been made were not of an intimate kind. The plans of King George IV to make a pleasure garden around Royal Lodge, just beyond the Copper Horse, had been abandoned a hundred years previously and the paling erected to keep out the deer, which roamed the Park until the Second World War, had been removed for routine maintenance purposes at the Castle. But in 1931 (Sir) Eric Savill took up his post of Deputy Surveyor of Parks and Woods and began to think of indulging his taste for gardening on some of the land within his care. Before Percy's time at Windsor was over a start had been made on the great Savill Garden and the preliminary works, although far outside the kind of gardening the bothy boys knew, were there to be seen by people walking in the Park. In the same year, 1931, the Duke and Duchess of York, later King George VI and Queen Elizabeth, became the tenants of Royal Lodge. They shared an interest in gardening and were soon developing their surroundings. Aided by the Duchess's favourite and youngest brother, (Sir) David Bowes Lyon, their new friendship with Savill, and later the greatest landscape gardener of this century, (Sir) Geoffrey Jellicoe, they made it in due time the most celebrated of Queen Elizabeth's several much-loved gardens. It was the sort of garden where the bothy boys could perhaps hope to be head one day. Meanwhile, there were years of grind to be gone through, knowledge and experience to be gained, and the ladder of the garden hierarchy to be climbed.

As a royal establishment the Windsor gardens harboured a number of men, many of them crippled or reduced by the First World War, who would not have found employment elsewhere. They were the sort of people whom the Royal Household, and its microcosm the Royal Gardens, traditionally found room for on full pay in jobs which recognized their limitations. But the rest of the staff, in their five grades, were the cream of the profession. Next to Charles Cook were the five foremen, each with his own establishment and equipment, and each exercising as much responsibility as a head gardener at most private houses. The same could be said of the three specialist growers – for carnations, orchids and chrysanthemums. Below them came the journeymen and last, with Percy among them, the improvers.

Percy's first foreman was called Waltham, and he had charge of the fruit houses. Waltham was an old acquaintance of Harry Thrower, with whom he had worked at King's Waldenbury, and somewhat similar in character, though he seems to have had more time to ensure that his standards were realized under his personal supervision. Percy was not allowed to do anything by himself. He was attached to a journeyman and instructed to follow him around, with Waltham appearing at regular intervals to check up on both of them. Like Harry Thrower, Waltham kept all the pruning to himself and even after he had advanced to journeyman Percy would merely be detailed to stand behind him and follow on doing the tying up. Waltham did entrust the training of fruit trees to lesser hands, no doubt because any damage done through ignorance could be relatively easily undone. Only one standard was acceptable and that was perfection. Fan-training a peach tree could easily take a whole day and if at the end of it the job was not to Waltham's standards he would order it to be done again.

The days for such prodigality with time, labour and money were, alas, numbered, as were those for large-scale hot-house fruit growing at all. Literally anything could be produced in abundance and to a required date in the hot-houses, provided there was money to pay for the heating and for months of highly-skilled care. In Percy's early years at Shrewsbury after the Second World War the annual Flower Show still included large exhibits of indoor fruit from a handful of houses such as Mentmore, but they disappeared in the early 1950s. At Windsor twenty years before the hot-houses were still working at full strength, supplying not only Windsor but Buckingham Palace and anywhere else that the Court happened to be, although at Sandringham a more modest version of the Windsor gardens kept the house partly supplied.

The fruit houses at Windsor consisted of houses for cucumbers, melons and strawberries, and two fruit ranges, each a quarter of a mile long and divided into four, one part for each season of the year. Apples and other less demanding fruits were grown in orchards towards the boundary of the gardens where they adjoined those of Frogmore House. In such circumstances there was comparatively little need to give much attention to forcing, although ripe strawberries had to be ready for the Court's customary arrival at Windsor for Easter. Fruit ready for consumption had to leave the gardens and reach its destination, whether up at the Castle or further afield, in perfect condition. Not so much as a finger mark on a ripe peach would pass, although there were benefits to be had because rejects, like windfalls, were one of the bothy boys' few perks.

As far as the bothy boys were concerned, Charles Cook sometimes had a softer, human side. Whistling was apparently tolerated in the glasshouses. Percy was once surprised at his work by Cook, standing misty-eyed behind him and asking, 'Excuse me, old boy, what's that tune you're whistling?' It was Waldteufel's 'Skater's Waltz', which Percy had heard in a dance-hall. 'Ah, yes,' said Cook, stepping backwards, 'Yes, of course. We had one gramophone record in the trenches and we played it over and over again. That was it.' Thereafter, the head gardener was never quite so unlike other men again.

Smoking, on the other hand, was totally forbidden at work. While at Windsor Percy was going through the Woodbine phase, in which a modest satisfaction could be achieved in a very short time, if necessary while going off to have a pee. Percy had tried his father's pipe when a small boy and it had made him disgustingly sick. The consequent aversion to pipes lasted for twenty years, after which he gradually became a continuous, deep pipe smoker until the very last years of his life. Smoking at work had been forbidden at Horwood too, but in that more relaxed world it was not such a crime and could be quite easily explained away. Thus, if Mrs Denny came in unexpectedly and asked 'What's that smell?', the reply, 'Just fumigating, Mrs Denny,' would send her away uncomplaining. Cook, however, knew this trick. Working alone in the vinery one day, giving the vines a tar-oil wash, Percy heard the great man's tread upon the iron grating that covered the hot water pipes in the floor of the doorway, and was discovered with one foot nailed to the floor on top of a fag-end and a wraith of blue smoke drifting towards an open light. The situation was mildly embarrassing for Cook as well because he had a visitor with him and had no wish to dramatize the obvious lapse in discipline by making a scene in front of him. Instead, he raised his nose and sniffed, like a bull appraising his cows, and as he lowered his heels enquired: 'Thrower! Someone been fumigating with nicotine in here?' The question withered Percy like a sharp early frost.

Percy had very particular reasons to aspire to the head gardener's approval. Against all the rules he had become deeply attached to his elder daughter, Connie. It was common knowledge in the bothy that this devotion was to some degree reciprocated and because of it the boys decided that he must be destined for great things – provided he did not get himself hanged meanwhile.

During Percy's first two years at Windsor Connie had left school and done a secretarial course. Now she had got a job at the Westminster Bank in Slough and bicycled there daily from home. In so far as her parents had thought at all about her marriage prospects they had perhaps hoped that she would marry someone from the bank.

The bothy boys were somewhat inhibited by their circumstances from making much progress with girls. They lived in common, had relatively little free time and were dreadfully short of cash for taking girls out and about. From time to time they were confined to the gardens at weekends or for a succession of evenings while they took their turn in attending to the routine and never-ending jobs of watering, adjusting the ventilation and so on. Out on the town there was alarming competition, for the population of Windsor was permanently swollen by the Foot Guards and the Household Cavalry in the three barracks spread across the southern side of the town.

The presence of the army was as much of a dilemma to Connie's parents as to the bothy boys, for the common and licentious soldiery of the town must be a far greater menace than the garden men kept literally under one's own lock and key. The society of the Royal Household itself was already incestuous and, typically of all small closed worlds, it was peculiarly difficult to take a step upwards within it. Mrs Cook, very sensibly realizing that nothing would probably keep her daughters and the bothy boys apart, decided that they should best meet on her own terms. The girls saw the matter differently. 'There were at least twenty healthy young men in that bothy,' Connie's sister Mabel recalled. 'One way or another we were going to get to know them.'

As part of their job the Cooks were responsible for organizing dances or whist drives at which their daughters would require, in the most proper sense, escorts. And so the more presentable bothy boys were sent for. More informal encounters could be engineered, when Connie was going to or returning from work, for example, or on Sunday evenings when she frequently went to Evensong in the parish church without her parents. Her parents usually went to St George's Chapel, where Charles Cook had a stall which went with his job. Forty years later, when opening the Datchet Horticultural Show, Percy said he was particularly fond of the place because he had done most of his courting there. Datchet, though only just across the Thames from the Royal Gardens, was outside the gardeners' usual territory. Even so, by the time he left Windsor in 1935, Percy and Connie were no more than close friends. There could be no question of marriage until he was eligible for a job with a house, and the only way to that was through more and even better work.

After two years in the fruit houses Percy was transferred to the plant houses and promoted to journeyman. Here he had some independence and responsibility at last, and with certain species was working directly with the specialist growers. The foreman was a small man named Hale who, overblown and corrupted by a lot of power in a small world, was something of a bully, though not towards Percy. His favourite butts were those who were already accident prone and his handling of them amused the other men at least. For most of his life Percy was fond of recalling with glee Hale's handling of one youth who appeared one morning, not for the first time, clutching his side in apparent agony:

'What's the matter with you then this morning?'

'Oh, Gawd! I've got such a pain here.'

'I think it's tubrick you've got, my lad.'

'Tubrick? What's that, Mr Hale, what's that?'

'It's confused wind. Your face is so much like your backside that the wind don't know which way to turn!'

The plant houses were where royalty was most likely to be seen, but not in any circumstances encountered. Like the Dennys at Horwood, King George V and Queen Mary often visited the plant houses on Sunday mornings, between mattins and luncheon. The basic instruction to Percy and the others was to make themselves scarce when royalty approached, and if that was impossible to try to pretend they were not there. Conversations overheard could cast light on the breadth of the royal mind, as when Queen Mary came upon some anthuriums. 'Cook! Have these taken away. Terribly rude-looking things!' (Indeed, with their shiny red flowers and protruding spathes they are rather alarming.) Lesser royalty, such as the knee-high princesses Elizabeth and Margaret picking daffodils at Frogmore, could at least return a wave.

Queen Mary's taste in flower colours was the opposite of Mrs Denny's. Where Mrs Denny rejoiced in strong colours in strong mixtures, the Queen preferred pastel shades and thus loved certain varieties of fuchsia. Fuchsias were not then a popularly grown plant, nor were they to become so until after the Second World War, but Percy made note of Queen Mary's liking for them.

King George's one unchanging and absolute floral requirement was a daily gardenia, fresh and ready for him to put in his buttonhole after breakfast, wherever he might be. If all the miles of hot pipes and acres of glass at the Royal Gardens had one fundamental reason for existing, the King's gardenia was it. It was immaculate when placed upon the breakfast table but once there might be pecked over or even destroyed by the King's marauding parrot, Charlotte, a privileged bird whose welfare featured in ministerial telegrams and memoranda. The King would acknowledge no fault in her. The present Earl of Harewood recalls her perched on his knee when he was still in short trousers and he beginning to wince and fidget as she tightened her not inconsiderable grip, and his grandfather saying: 'Tell the boy to sit still. He's frightening Charlotte.'

The most hectic time of the year in the plant houses was Ascot Week when there was the Royal Box at the racecourse to be decorated and routine flower arrangements for the large party at the Castle, as well as special events such as the Waterloo Day Dinner on 18 June, which very frequently fell during the same week. This dinner is given in honour of the first Duke of Wellington and his victory at the Battle of Waterloo; it is the occasion when the current duke, his descendant, hands the monarch the nominal rent for Stratfield Saye, the house and estate near Reading with which the first duke was rewarded. Their work done – with a floral scheme based on gold if the eighteenth happened to be Gold Cup Day – the garden staff were allowed to stay and have a discreet look at the proceedings. Apart from the King and Queen there would be few faces they would recognize, except perhaps Eric Savill, in court breeches instead of his customary plus-fours.

The real pleasure of Ascot Week, however, was going over to the course to decorate the Royal Box and parts of the Enclosure, with quite a lot of free time to follow. The 5.30 a.m. start for Ascot, shaven and open-eyed as on any other day, was no particular hardship in midsummer as the normal start of work was only an hour later. The decorations at Ascot were based on a profusion of roses in scented varieties, with masses of foliage and banks of shrubs, especially hydrangeas, brought over in pots. They were supposed to be finished by 9.30, when the men were rewarded with bread and cheese and beer. From then until after the end of the day's racing, when it was time to clear up, they were free to enjoy a day's racing alongside everybody else.

With the help of a knowledgeably marked card Percy's first day at the races was an intoxicating success, and although the turf came to take second place to other forms of gambling he never entirely lost his taste for it, though he never won or lost much either way. Years later, at intervals during a horticultural show at which he was judging, he would disappear to search for a friendly television and news of the day's form. His first killing was on a horse ridden by Gordon Richards.

Institutions like the Royal Gardens can be all-embracing and constantly reassuring, so that after a while there can be little incentive to move on. But the Depression was beginning to affect even Windsor and the prospects of advancement there, never good, dwindled out of sight. Beside the ambition to rise and to marry, Percy quite simply wanted to gain experience of gardening elsewhere, on different soil, in a different climate, with different tastes and requirements to satisfy. There were a handful of private house gardens still going strong, but not to the extent of actually wanting to take on extra men. There were a few great gardens belonging to the new rich but they, as Percy well understood, could disappear as quickly as they had sprung up. The one area of stability, if not of actual growth, was municipal gardening. Percy made enquiries of contacts among the seed salesmen, the grapevines for such information, and one of them came up with a vacancy for a journeyman in the City of Leeds Parks Department. He duly got the job, and in the summer of 1935, with great regret and some dread, prepared to move north.

As it happened, there was little short of a revolution in the gardens at Windsor within eighteen months of his departure. The death of King George V in January 1936 was the end of an era in the history of English Court life which had begun with the reform of the Royal Household by Prince Albert in the 1850s. The new King, Edward VIII, took an attitude that was at once more brisk and more relaxed. Then in the spring after George V's death Wallis Simpson visited the Royal Gardens and cast a predatory eye upon the peach blossom, which she wanted for decorative use. Charles Cook, who cannot have been asked such a question seriously before, merely said: 'Madam, these are fruiting trees. They must not be cut.' The King himself was perplexed by all the abundance, of the fruit houses in particular, and is said to have asked: 'I can't eat all this fruit. Why should anybody else?'

Charles Cook was spared the worst by Queen Mary's sensitivity and love of what she knew. Tom Cook, Charles's brother and counterpart at Sandringham, retired and Queen

Mary quickly removed the other Cooks to take his place there. He was to be head gardener at Sandringham until 1952 – for slightly longer in fact than he had served at Windsor. On the February morning of the death of King George VI, one of his very last jobs was to assemble some flowers and place them beside the body.

3

Leeds and Derby

Percy left Windsor on 1 August 1935. Asked to spot the gardener in an identity parade nobody would have chosen him. His hair was fashionably brilliantined, he wore a suit and a trilby hat (or sometimes a bowler when Charles Cook was not looking); he had a brisk – almost sharp – manner in giving or taking instructions which, though in fact one of the hallmarks of a good royal servant, might have suggested to an outsider that he was someone on the way up in business. Beneath this exterior he had in reality less experience of life in general than most people in their twenty-third year. On the day he left Windsor there was much to make him uneasy and not a little to make him positively discontented. He would be living for the first time outside a community based on a large house and, furthermore, living in the north of England; he was leaving Connie with nothing understood, let alone agreed, between them.

Anywhere north of Little Horwood was not entirely foreign country to him. He had spent holidays visiting gardens with his parents and these had included Castle Kennedy in Scotland, where the head gardener was an old family friend. Castle Kennedy, however, was an acknowledged near paradise which would survive serenely in almost any age. Leeds, with all the other grim cities of the north, was just a collection of Victorian relics, and from any point of view more promising ground for a J. B. Priestley or a George Orwell than for a municipal gardener. The story of the times was told through the carriage window during Percy's journey north, through disused branch lines leading to roofless factories and by the out-of-date advertisements on the station walls.

The City of Leeds had no guide book and no tourists. It was Victorian and parochial. 'An individualist,' Sir John Betjeman wrote, 'would not understand it.' The imposing houses of the manufacturers in the leafy suburbs had long been deserted when their owners retired, usually southwards, to a gentler life. The huge, galleried churches which their great-grandfathers had built as proof of their good works were soot-encrusted and locked. The dark brown Aire and Calder Canal seethed with microbial life. Of the poor who remained, there were only those who were so poor that they could not afford to move elsewhere. In 1935 Leeds led the nation in having the largest proportion of the population living in back-to-back houses. The people were said to be friendly. Sharing a clothes-line, slung from front bedroom to front bedroom, they could scarcely not be at least on speaking terms.

Percy learnt more about the unemployed of Leeds from the people with whom he lodged, the Claughtons. He was an out-of-work brass fitter and his wife, on whom typically enough the burden of this disaster fell, took in two lodgers to keep themselves going. Mrs Claughton had been cook to Lord Halifax at Temple Newsam, so her family and the lodgers fared very well in the circumstances. Percy was never the sort of man who would need to darn his own socks if there was a woman around and one way and another was soon comfortable enough. The Claughtons' house was in Halton, three miles from the city centre. Even so, when a fog descended in the November after Percy's arrival, it was like something just before the end of the world to one unfamiliar to life in an industrial city, and bicycling through it left crusts of black around the eyes and nostrils.

Whatever the facts of its situation, the City of Leeds had never been short of civic pride and it had been swollen by a royal visit to open the new Civic Hall in August 1933. The authorities had already started to do something to improve the appalling houses, although at the rate of progress shown by 1933 it would have taken something like two hundred years to clear all the back-to-back terraces. Meanwhile, end-less committees deliberated on such cosmetic questions as the nomenclature of the streets, trying to decide whether the day for the Stipendiary streets, the Gas streets, the Industrial streets and even the Back Cemetery lanes, might be done. Expenditure on parks and gardens, and on more ephemeral forms of floral display, might, like the churches and chapels before them, enjoy high public approval.

Percy owed his job at Leeds to this expansionist mood, and was put to work in one of the city's more recent acquisitions, Temple Newsam Park. The house had been bought with 917 acres in 1922 from the first Earl of Halifax, who was later Viceroy of India. The superb house has much in common, in both date and appearance, with Hatfield House in Hertford-shire; but Temple Newsam is further ennobled by its elevated position, a setting made much of by Capability Brown, although it must be said that landscapes attributed to Brown are about as numerous as beds in which Elizabeth I slept. The most ambitious of the several gardens at the house seems to have been the Jacobean one laid out by the Frenchman Peter Monjoye, with its elaborately geometrical pattern of flower-beds, walks of pleached trees and exotic topiary matching carved stone beasts. The eighteenth-century landscapers brought the park right up to the walls of the house

47

and contrived a prospect limited only by the horizon. The Victorians brought the immediate environs of the house back into cultivation by establishing formal flower-beds. Until the last years of Lord Halifax's ownership it had been a country house in full working order; there was even a bothy. The work on which Percy was engaged was that of turning a private, country-house garden into a public park.

The works begun in the mid-1930s have now grown to include a herb garden, a spring garden, and – with a backward look – an Italian garden of box, yew and beech hedges, with formal flower-beds and walks of pleached laburnum, an arboretum, and a bog garden.

After its acquisition of Temple Newsam, the city authorities made much use of the glasshouses and other service buildings that remained in the kitchen garden from its days as a private house. Evidence of the more ample times, which reminded Percy of Windsor, were to be found here and there, such as the tall fire wall dated 1788 in the long conservatory, pierced by flues to conduct air to ripen pineapples and other fruit.

Percy was growing in expertise as a glasshouse specialist and much of his time at Leeds was given to the preparation of the bedding and other plants which were needed for planting out in the city centre and parks, and for floral decoration of the town and civic halls on a day-to-day basis as well as for formal occasions. One of the aspects of gardening at Leeds which perplexed Percy after his experience at Horwood and Windsor was the needless waste. Although Windsor, in particular, produced as much as could be expected of a garden, no waste was tolerated there and the maximum and most imaginative use was made of everything through cuttings, over-wintering, division and recycling. At Leeds they would have none of this. Hundreds of thousand of bulbs would be

Percy's parents, Beatrice and Harry
Thrower, in the kitchen garden at
Horwood House, Buckinghamshire
(*Mrs Maude Seaton*).

Inset: the head gardener's house, Percy's
home for the first eighteen years of his
life.

Percy, aged six months, with his parents and elder brother Harry, outside the head gardener's house, Horwood.

The *étang*, Horwood House *(inset)*, with trees from the garden of the former Rectory House beyond *(Country Life)*.

Percy, aged eleven. He was a lively and mischievous little boy with a liking for practical jokes.

Harry Thrower in the kitchen garden at Horwood with giant Himalayan lilies, the result of a visit to Castle Kennedy in Scotland.

The head gardener's house, Windsor, where Connie Cook (later Mrs Percy Thrower) and her sister lived with their parents. 'Keep your eyes off the head gardener's daughters!' Percy was told.

Percy stands proudly outside the 'bothy' in the Royal Gardens at Windsor. The young gardeners lived in common here and getting a place was quite an achievement.

Like his father before him, Percy loved shooting. It was his only recreation, and he enjoyed it to the very end of his life. Here he is at Horwood on holiday from Windsor where he started work as an 'improver' in 1931.

Left: Percy while at Derby in the late 1930s. Here he inspects a cyclamen, one of the species with which, like his father, he excelled.

Percy at work in the nursery. No flat cap for him!

Although only six days after the outbreak of the Second World War, Percy and Connie's wedding went ahead as planned. From left: Percy's parents, Beatrice and Harry, Joan (sister) and Harry (brother), Percy, Connie, Connie's father, Charles, Mabel (sister) and Connie's mother, Ina.

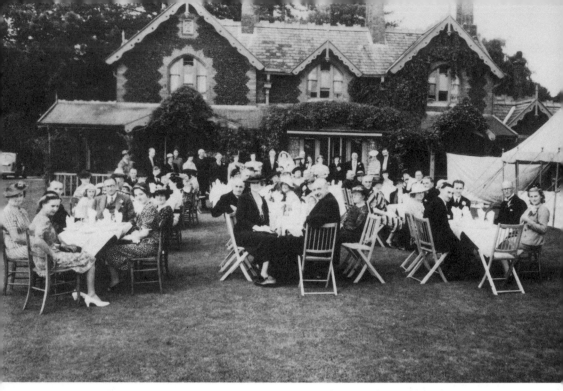

9 September 1939: over 100 people enjoy Percy and Connie's wedding reception on the lawn of Connie's father's house at Sandringham (*Mrs Maude Seaton*).

The war found Percy leading the 'dig for victory' campaign at Derby. *Inset:* Barely recognizable, Percy as a special constable in wartime Derby. The Morris 8 was bought on a football pools win.

lifted every year and buried or burnt, followed in the autumn by shrubs brought to maturity at Temple Newsam and destroyed after one season's display in the town. A small proportion of them planted out to take their chance on the waste ground which abounded might have given tremendous pleasure in an otherwise joyless scene; but the city fathers much preferred licensed waste to the risk of pilfering and the idea that a handful of bulbs might end up in some journeyman's back garden.

The young journeyman Percy did not go unnoticed in Leeds. Several respectable matrons still living there have recently recalled that at the end of their schooldays they would go for walks in Temple Newsam Park in the hope that Percy might look up from his work and smile at them or even say 'Good afternoon'. Percy's instincts, however, were absorbed elsewhere. Every weekend he wrote to Connie, long letters in tiny handwriting covering the minutiae of his work and way of life, the contrasts with Windsor, and the particular problems of gardening in a heavily industrialized atmosphere.

In the airy retreat of Temple Newsam, a few miles southeast of the city centre, or at Harewood House a little further out to the north, large specimen trees flourished in the parkland. It was not so nearer the city itself, where sulphureous deposits gradually killed off trees which might otherwise have stood for centuries. The will to make Leeds a more inhabitable place through the provision of public parks and gardens was certainly strong but conditions were very hostile until something was done to purify the air a generation later.

The benefits of large open spaces in cities for the good of the body, and later the soul, had long been understood. The earliest and most earnest propagandists had been Germans, and the Tiergarten in Berlin was made available for the people to walk in by the middle of the seventeenth century; Moorfields in London was improved with the same function in mind a few years later. Sometimes the remains of fortifications, planted with avenues of trees, made excellent natural promenades. The use of the Roman earthworks at Dorchester for this purpose were well described in the 1880s in Thomas Hardy's novel *The Mayor of Casterbridge*. Where no such amenities were available, the people were often encouraged to take the air in the cemeteries. The idea was taken a stage further in Germany in the first half of the nineteenth century with the idea of the 'Volksgarten'. These were not for the enjoyment of the open air alone; the ideal was that: 'Buildings with interesting pictures from the history of the nation, statues of their dead heroes and monuments to important events with instructive inscriptions can be tastefully arranged at appropriate places to very advantageous effect.' Prince Albert sought to realize this vision in Kensington Gardens.

Prince Albert had been preceded as an advocate of public parks in this country by John Claudius Loudon (1783–1843) who, after extensive travels in Europe, concluded that: 'Our continental neighbours have hitherto excelled us in this department of gardening; almost every town of consequence having its promenades for the citizens *en cheval* and also *au pied*. Till lately Hyde Park, at London, and a spot called "The Meadows", near Edinburgh were the only equestrian gardens in Britain; and neither were well arranged.' Some of the royal parks, pre-eminently Hyde Park, had long been open to all, but some of the later parks, including Regent's Park, which was newly laid-out when Loudon wrote, really only catered for the rich and did not acknowledge the existence of pedestrians.

Percy was later to find at Shrewsbury the combination of public open space and pleasure garden which the Victorian improvers preferred. There the Quarry and the Dingle within it had been established by a mixture of custom, public philanthropy and private imagination. But it was at Derby, where Percy moved – still a journeyman – early in 1937, that the first municipal arboretum in England had been opened in 1840.

The twelve or so acres on which the Derby Arboretum was made had been given to the town for the purpose in the early nineteenth century by a local philanthropist, Joseph Strutt, and Loudon was commissioned to design it. Loudon approved of the well-drained site but not of the view, which he rightly thought lacked anything worth looking at. To close off unpleasing views he had mounds no more than about ten feet high thrown up at strategic points. This technique would have been familiar to any eighteenth-century landscape designer; but in other respects Loudon moved away from the cult of the picturesque in favour of a style of planting which he called 'gardenesque', and aimed to allow each plant or tree to develop its natural character as fully as possible. The lay-out of the Arboretum meant that it could be walked through or strolled around, and ample provision was made for the people to sit and think, free of charge.

By the late 1930s the Arboretum contained a considerable heritage of mature trees and shrubs. Yet when Percy was working there just before the war, contrary to the hopes of Strutt and Loudon and the civic authorities then and since, it was singularly difficult to get the public actually to go in and enjoy it. Even on the finest days the Arboretum would be all but deserted, apart from a gaggle or so of quarrelling children and a few old men asleep in the sun. A great deal of trouble and money was consequently spent on bringing flowers to the

51

people in the streets, in hanging baskets and in window-boxes. Some of the nursery work was done in the Arboretum but most of it was carried out north of the town at Darley Abbey which, like Temple Newsam, had been a private house whose gardens were in the process of being turned into a public park.

The former head gardener at Darley Abbey, John Maxfield, had been absorbed by the Derby Parks Department and was still in charge when Percy went to work there. He was, in Percy's recollection, very probably the best head gardener he ever encountered. He could judge from a man's posture, gait and hands whether or not he was going to be any good. A watering can properly handled was the mark of acceptability in Maxfield's eyes. Did he water simply for the sake of watering, or because he had tapped a pot and heard that the plant actually needed watering? Did he slop water around from a half-filled can, or fill and empty a can methodically? And so on. Maxfield's cyclamen and begonias left even Harry Thrower's standing for well-founded vigour and floriferous abundance. He was no martinet and would occasionally go as far as deferring to Percy on some detail of garden practice. But far more than gestures of that kind Percy treasured his rare, dry compliment: 'You're not doing too bad.'

While at Derby Percy began to spread himself a little social-ly. He made friends outside the restricted circle of the Parks Department, and arranged some regular rough shooting for himself on a farm on the outskirts of the town. At work, although he had advanced to foreman and, before he left Derby, was to become assistant parks superintendent, he was beginning to strain for real authority in ways which often manifestly irritated the superintendent himself. He was very well liked by the men, which was just as well because none of them was allowed to go home at the end of the day without his permission. He used his trilby hat almost as a badge of rank, although for some reason it was ceremoniously removed when he was engaged in potting on.

None of this cut much ice when he went over to Sandringham to visit Connie and her parents shortly after they had moved there from Windsor. Mrs Cook rather implied that she had not expected ever to see him again and that his reappearance was not an occasion of pleasure to her. Charles Cook, on the other hand, was rather more welcoming, perhaps out of curiosity in the knowledge that he would clearly soon have to think of Percy as a colleague, albeit in an inferior arm of their profession, rather than as a junior employee. For Connie the visit was a mixture of pleasure and apprehension: pleasure at seeing the man behind the tiny handwriting again; apprehension at what she must presently tell her parents of the understanding that had been established between them.

4

Marriage and the War

Percy and Connie became engaged in the course of 1938. Once things between them reached this stage, the Cooks' attitude changed. If they had any regrets that Connie had not chosen to do 'better' than a municipal gardener for a husband, these were subsumed by a desire to have the marriage ceremony and reception done in style. Before the Second World War had become a probability rather than a possibility, it had been decided that the wedding should be on the second Saturday in September 1939, during a season of comparative quiet in the gardens at Derby and Sandringham.

The declaration of war on Sunday 3 September threw these cherished plans into confusion. Well over one hundred people had been invited to the wedding in Sandringham Church and the reception at the head gardener's house, which, unlike its counterpart at Windsor, had more of the atmosphere of a rectory than an official residence. East Anglia, however, is more directly exposed to Germany than anywhere else in this country and was not a part of the world in which many people might choose to spend the first Saturday of the war. A postponement was seriously considered, but in the end Charles Cook decided that everything should go ahead as far as practicable according to plan, although it was far from clear whether everybody – even Percy's parents – would be able to get there. Percy had to arrange a substitute best man lest his brother Harry, the first choice for the role, could not get there either.

The realities of the phoney war had yet to sink in, however, and on the great day everything and everybody came together, not unduly flushed or bothered. The church choir turned out at full strength, with the incumbent of Sandringham, a chaplain to the King, resplendent in red. Percy had been induced to wear a morning suit, though he never relished dressing-up, even after he had become an active Freemason, or for that matter dressing-down for the garden either. Both sets of parents looked remarkably proud and pleased in the photographs.

Percy and Connie, like millions of other bridal couples, looked shy and slightly apprehensive, restrained from actually looking happy by the solemnity of the occasion. In later years, Percy claimed that he could remember very little about it all, except that Connie looked lovely. She was slightly darker than her husband, with an enviable figure which she kept through childbearing or the passage of time; like him, she had eyes that were blue and arrestingly steady. If Percy really could not remember that Connie wore a dress of ivory satin, with an embroidered veil held in place by an orange blossom chaplet, he certainly remembered her bouquet of lilies and carnations, together with the pink carnations and blue scabious of the two bridesmaids' bouquets, which went with their dresses of blue crêpe de Chine.

After a bibulous afternoon on the Cooks' lawn, Percy and Connie went off to Derby, taking some left-overs to see them through what remained of the weekend. There was no honeymoon because all leave had been cancelled in the Parks Department and Percy was due to return to work on Monday morning. Such, so the psychologists of these matters say, is the best way of celebrating and beginning a marriage.

Thus Connie – a year Percy's junior in age but further

behind even him in terms of experience – was cast into life in wartime Derby. Percy had decided when he left Horwood in 1931 that he would always be self-sufficient and never resort, even in emergencies, to his parents for financial help, and he had done remarkably well in setting up house ready for Connie's arrival. In accordance with the commendable standards and expectations of those days he would not seriously have asked Connie to marry him if he had not been in a position to provide for her and support her.

Somehow over the previous four years he had saved enough money to furnish and make habitable a semi-detached house. The furniture was mainly basic household necessities, but included an *art deco* bedroom suite in walnut. There were also of course wedding presents too to help them on their way. As Connie quickly discovered, to her surprise and mild disappointment, Percy, though capable of making anything flourish in the garden, had the hand of death with any work within the house, even something as simple as putting in a reliable screw. Some of the presents that had to be put up became casualties of this disability. Queen Mary's present of a set of Burslem dishes was far too precious to be put on any shelf of Percy's making and mercifully survived and remained throughout the marriage of nearly fifty years.

The house was rented. House-ownership had no place in the way of life to which both Connie and Percy had been born and bred; neither was it in tune with the mood of the time. Who would have wanted to buy a house in wartime Derby? The sad fact was, of course, that because nobody wanted to buy a house in Derby, the one which the Throwers rented could easily have been bought very cheaply, albeit on a mortgage, which was now well within Percy's means. Although Percy later came to regret that he had not made the investment then, he was partly discouraged at the time by the realization that buying the house would somehow suggest that Derby was as far as he was going in his career. But rather more telling was the fact that Derby, as a centre for engineering and the manufacture of a wide range of armaments and machines of war, suffered a full share of bombing. In those circumstances, almost as much as at the front in battle, the mind is concentrated on living on a very short time scale. Percy twice volunteered for the forces but was sent back because of the nature of his work. Nevertheless, Connie lived with the menace of his possible call-up during the early years of their marriage. The uncertainty, which made every day without the call-up something of a bonus, prolonged the honeymoon and added an intensity to the happiness of their early married life. There were aspects of service life that Percy would undoubtedly have enjoyed because he always relished the atmosphere of a disciplined organization. When, one by one, many of his contemporaries at Derby went off to war he was frequently at the station to bid them farewell, in a state of excitement which some of them mistook for glee at seeing them go.

Neither of Percy's brothers saw any action in the field. Harry, who was by now in 'service' in London, joined the auxiliary ambulance brigade; Maurice, who was in the Ordnance Corps, never had to go abroad. One personal loss they all suffered during the war was due to other causes. Percy's father died, quite suddenly, on 31 December 1939 from a haemorrhage of the lungs earlier that day. From the days when Percy could first remember his father he had been liable to go purple in the face during paroxysms of coughing brought on by his pipe. He smoked, in the fullest sense, an ounce of tobacco a day (a half of what Percy himself eventually

58

came to consume). His condition was made worse, when the gardens at Horwood were decaying around him, by having to spend a fair amount of his time in the sulphureous world of the boiler house, struggling to keep things going with an impossibly depleted staff.

Percy and Connie themselves were on several occasions perilously close to disaster. The noise of war and the sounds of bombs became part of daily life, and of nights spent on a mattress under the dining-room table. Yet ordinary life went on. Percy had passed the Royal Horticultural Society's General Examination while still at Leeds, and was now working towards the National Diploma in Horticulture. Towards the end of the war he went to Wisley to take part of the examination and stopped over for a night in London with his brother Harry. The night was sleepless because of an air raid. This was the era of buzz-bombs, when the worst part was the unnatural silence between the engines cutting out and the bomb exploding. During that interval there was no way of knowing whether or not the bomb was heading straight for one. Percy's failure in the examination at this first attempt (he passed it later), was due less to a bad night than to an exercise towards the end which frequently foxed the sharpest candidates. This question consisted of being shown a selection of weeds, categorizing them botanically, and then reciting their uses.

The unfortunate Connie spent many of her nights under the table alone and often saw precious little of Percy during the days either. As the people's war cranked itself into action he became involved on three fronts: as a special constable, on fire-watching duty, and in helping to organize the 'Dig for Victory' effort in Derby and the surrounding area.

Fire-watching was by far the most demanding of these jobs.

It was frequently hazardous and was done at night, after a normal day's work. When on duty in the town centre, naps could be snatched in the Turkish bath. Next to a pub with no beer, nowhere is more unwelcoming than a cold Turkish bath in the dark. Fortunately Percy had inherited a facility to have a sleep, brief but sound, after luncheon every day irrespective of where he was or what he was doing, and nothing was allowed to interfere with it. He could remain infuriatingly lively throughout a hard wartime night, and the habit was later to sustain him through impossibly heavy work schedules in peace.

Patrolling the Arboretum one night with Ken Hodgkinson, a newcomer to the parks who later became a distinguished superintendent, the pair were literally surrounded by falling bombs. The first of them, far too close for comfort, caused them to freeze before falling instinctively on their faces under a tree with Percy on top, as five bombs came down into the Arboretum itself. Hodgkinson believed, then and later, that Percy had saved his life. Nevertheless, he was still dazed when Percy had him on his feet and at work clearing up, in particular improvising cover for plants suddenly exposed to the cold night air. Before their emergency efforts had gone very far there was news that the bombing had been particularly heavy in the London Road area of Derby, where Percy lived. He rushed back to find Connie blanched and shaken, and their house with the windows blown out and the ceiling down, but mercifully that was all.

Percy's principal occupation during the war was organizing the 'Dig for Victory' effort. He was clearly unusually good at it and it was largely responsible for his accelerated progress through the ranks from foreman, to general foreman and finally assistant superintendent. It developed, trained and exercised skills that he was later to use on an audience of millions on television.

The slogan 'Dig for Victory' was originally the sub-title of the 'Grow More Food Campaign' launched in August 1939. It was popularized by the Minister of Agriculture in a wireless broadcast two months later:

> We want not only the big man with the plough but the little man with the spade to get busy this autumn. . . . Let 'Dig for Victory' be the motto of everyone with a garden. . . . Half a million more allotments properly worked will provide potatoes and vegetables that will feed another million adults and one and half million children for eight months of the year, so let's get going and let 'Dig for Victory' be the matter for everyone with a garden or allotment and every man and woman capable of digging an allotment in their spare time.

Gardening came close to being turned into a martial art by popularizing some lines from Andrew Marvell's poem 'The Garden of Appleton House, Laid out by Lord Fairfax in Figure of a Fort':

> *See how the flowers, as at parade,*
> *Under their colours stand display'd:*
> *Each regiment in order grows,*
> *That of the tulip, pink and rose.*

Tremendous ingenuity was shown in getting the people gripped by the will to dig, and slogans abounded. The priestly appeal 'Lighten our Darkness' was punningly turned into 'Lighten our Ships', and 'Notes for Sermons' joined the torrent of propaganda issuing from the Ministry of Agriculture. A certain L. du Garde Peach, a name which would be implausible in fiction, wrote a wireless play with the title 'Dig for Victory'.

Lord Haw-Haw used to speak of the English digging their own graves, but the will to dig took root and the people dug. By 1943 the number of allotments kept had risen from its 1939 figure of 815,000 to 1,400,000. Rather more than half of all manual workers not on active service were said to be growing their own vegetables. The movement extended to livestock with the Domestic Poultry Keepers Council, which included rabbit-breeding for the table. By the end of the war there were nearly seven thousand pig clubs supervising the care of literally hundreds of thousands of pigs.

Allotments in the form that would be recognized now have existed in this country for at least two hundred years, ever since the bulk of the population began to move from its rural roots. They are ubiquitous but generally disregarded by all but their keepers. The late Harry Thorpe, Professor of Geography at Birmingham University, asked by the Wilson Government to report on the state and prospects of allotments in the late 1960s, brilliantly summarized what 'the allotment' conjured up for most people in some reflections published a few years later:

> . . . a rather sordid picture of a monotonous grid of rectangular plots, devoted mainly to vegetables and bush fruits, and tended by an older stratum of society, particularly men over forty, including many old-age pensioners. Prominent over many sites were assemblages of ramshackle huts, redolent of 'do it yourself', from the corrugated-iron roofs of which sagging down-spouting

carried rainwater into a motley collection of receptacles, long since rejected elsewhere, but again pressed into service here and ranging from antiquated baths to old zinc tanks and rusting oil drums. One in every five of the plots lay uncultivated, with weeds flourishing waist-high in summer, almost reaching the tops of abandoned bean-poles from which tattered pennants of polythene still fluttered noisily to scare birds from non-existent crops.

(The Homely Allotment: From Rural Dole to Urban Amenity: A Neglected Aspect of Urban Land Use', *Geography*, no. 268, vol. 60, part 3, July 1975)

Who has not seen them, usually beside the railway line in the middle suburbs of a large town, or some similarly unappealing spot? Land for allotments has seldom been designated because it was particularly suitable to harbour crops of vegetables and fruit, but because the sites were too small or difficult in shape or access for any other use.

Chance could throw up some wonderful allotment sites. Percy's first piece of land in the 'Dig for Victory' years was beside a sewage works, where the land can be not only fertile but fecund. Tomato pips, for example, are largely impervious to the digestive process and any sewage farm left to itself for a while would soon sprout a forest of tomato plants.

The sewage plant, with the racecourse, and parts of the public parks were among the sites made available to Percy for the 'Dig for Victory' effort. Each of the four Derby parks – Darley Abbey, the Arboretum, Alvaston Lake and Allestree – had a plot five hundred yards square, where Percy gave demonstrations and instructions to the new gardeners of wartime Britain. They were the old, and sometimes the very

young, the women and the partly sick in body and, sometimes, mind. The one thing they had in common was a
complete ignorance of gardening, whether from disincli-
nation, incapacity or lack of opportunity. Percy himself was
surprised at how easy it was to enthuse these people to master
the basic skills required for a degree of self-sufficiency. The
achievement was remarkable in that most of the effort was
given to growing bulky vegetables such as potatoes and
cabbage, often in the basic and less attractive varieties. Enthusiasm as well as improvidence could be enemies of the
effort. Some beginners, dissatisfied at the apparent lack of
progress of a crop after a week or two, would dig up what they
had planted to see what the matter was. There were also cases
of people eating the seed potatoes.

The digging instinct not only took root but took over. The
'Dig for Victory' scheme as such came to an end in 1951,
having been renamed 'Dig for Plenty' in the early years of
peace. Once it had answered the emergency, the legacy of the
scheme was in the instinct it rekindled: the feeling of every
individual's almost natural right to a piece of land on which to
grow food and on which to enjoy the pleasures of cultivated
nature on however small a scale. This was the instinct which it
fell to Percy, largely by accident, to nurture and develop in
ever more people during the more conspicuous part of his
career.

After a couple of seasons cabbages and potatoes in the
public parks became a normal part of the landscape. Nevertheless, in towns where the war had never been felt directly,
questions were asked at official levels about whether the 'Dig
for Victory' measures need continue. Could not the parks be
returned to their peacetime appearance? The work schedule
relaxed and Percy's vigour, refreshed by further and broader

experience, once again began to irritate the superintendent, T. S. Wells.

Although only just into his thirties Percy was more than ready for a superintendency of his own. It was a view that Wells shared for quite different reasons. Percy studied the trade and professional periodicals for vacancies but soon became used to Wells drawing his attention to them before he had had an opportunity to apply for any that sounded suitable or promising. The prizes for would-be superintendents in municipal gardening would be the posts at places such as Bath, or at southern resorts such as Torquay. In the last year of the war Percy was runner-up for the superintendency at Leamington Spa. That job went to George Ingle, a former colleague at Leeds, and at the time superintendent at Shrewsbury. His move left the Shrewsbury job vacant.

With peace, competition for the position was heavy. Seventy-two men applied, a few of them already superintendents in smaller towns, of whom nine were called to Shrewsbury for interview. Percy drove over from Derby the afternoon before his interview, with Connie, and also Margaret, their eldest daughter then eighteen months old, to stay overnight with a family called Ward, one of whom had been in charge at Shrewsbury before George Ingle. Mrs Elizabeth Ward, who had married into the family and was staying in the house awaiting her husband's demobilization, recalls that Percy seemed to be very nervous about the interview. The conversation over supper was mainly about 'Dig for Victory'; but later, describing how he and Connie had met, the royal connection inevitably came out, and from then on the Wards could not really see why Percy was worried about his chances. With Charles Cook (at that time still head gardener at Sandringham) for a father-in-law, Mrs Ward says:

'It seemed to us a certainty that the post would be his.'

'Connie', Mrs Ward recalls, 'was a lovely person; and I remember how dapper Percy looked at breakfast on the morning of the interview – in a morning suit! No doubt I had expected tweeds. Connie suddenly spotted a small hole in one of Percy's socks. Of course, I offered to darn it for him.'

Percy duly got the Shrewsbury job. His first and only ambition had been fulfilled at the age of thirty-two.

5

Shrewsbury

Percy took up office as parks superintendent at Shrewsbury on 1 January 1946. The prospect of the Quarry that raw morning was dispiriting. Among the weeds and piles of general rubbish were rows of cabbage stalks and old potato tops; in their mid-winter nakedness the rimy trees which made up the avenues of lime displayed all too painfully clearly their age and the distortion of their growth from being planted too close together. On this first morning Percy thought of his father and father-in-law on their first days as head gardeners. He might as well have thought of Capability Brown but, being a severely practical man, got down to work first.

'The Towne of Shrewsbury,' wrote the sixteenth-century topographer John Leland, 'standeth upon a Rocky Hill of Stone.' In addition to this naturally defensive character the town had a natural moat in the fast-flowing River Severn, which encompasses the whole town apart from a neck of land three hundred yards wide at the north-eastern approach from England. It was the sort of place that William the Conqueror might have entrusted to a fighting bishop but it went instead to his kinsman, Roger of Montgomery, who built the castle. The one thing which Shrewsbury lacks beside many places of its size, appearance and flavour is a medieval cathedral. Shrewsbury declined King Charles II's offer to make it a city. It is, nonetheless, a provincial metropolis, and, furthermore, it is quintessentially provincial. A large part of the rural West Midlands and mid-Wales looks to Shrewsbury; Shrewsbury itself does not look to London, partly no doubt because Birmingham is in the way. It has never, since the days of Elizabeth I, been conspicuously rich, but neither has it been uncomfortably poor: it is just prosperous, self-confident, and masonically inscrutable. The worthies of Shrewsbury have done very well by their open spaces.

'The Town of Flowers', as it has latterly been known, has more than 260 acres of parks and similar open spaces, pre-eminently the twenty-nine acres of the Quarry, which is surrounded by the River Severn on three sides, with the rich floral enclave of the Dingle in the middle. The Quarry was ancient common land used for grazing. In 1585 a man called Prince sowed barley on part of it and claimed the land as his own. Others followed his acquisitive example. To settle what had become a long-festering row, a bailiff bought out all who thought they had claims to the land and gave the whole to the town. One claimant to the use of the land refused to be bought out and for several generations his descendants claimed 4/6d a year in lieu of grazing. The Dingle, which is basically a large hollow, was the stone quarry itself and after it was exhausted declined into a bog or brackish pond depending on the weather or the time of year. The Quarry was a natural amphitheatre and a perfect setting for sports, pageants, rallies and military assemblies and exercises.

From 1719 a local benefactor and tree enthusiast, Thomas Wright, began planting the trees that became the celebrated avenues of limes in the Quarry. By the beginning of the nineteenth century they had a reputation as the finest lime avenues in Europe. The further refinement of the Quarry followed its use for the Shrewsbury Flower Show (at different times known under various permutations of 'Shrewsbury Musical and Floral Fête') in 1875. Although the show later achieved, and retains, a position amongst flower shows second only to Chelsea, its origin had much to do with the Victorian pursuit of refinement and lifting the eyes of farmers and burghers alike from the mire of daily life. It was begun 'specially for the fairer sex, whose more refined tastes would lead them to revel among the floral beauties, rather than wandering among cows and bulls and sheep and pigs, however much to be admired for their breeds and symmetry'.

In 1879 the handsome iron bandstand, with its ogee roof, was constructed between the Dingle and the Severn; the copy of the Farnese 'Hercules' was installed at the river end of the principal axial lime avenue; and the Dingle itself was made into a garden in a manner which has been likened to the picturesque grounds of a doll's house, with the 'gardenesque' style of planting applauded by Loudon. Percy could just remember it all in its pre-war finery from the days when family holidays had brought him to Shrewsbury when his father was judging in the show. But during the war the Dingle had reverted to a rat-infested boggy wilderness, and although the fine grass of the ploughed-up Quarry was dormant rather than extinct, it had all to be cultivated from scratch. Percy's job and the work required were not so far short of a completely new beginning.

Connie had also been to Shrewsbury as a child, in the wake of her father as a judge in the show, and had looked from the window of the main bedroom of Quarry Lodge at the fireworks which brought each year's event to a close. If the head gardener's house on a private estate was generally tucked away in some comfortable corner of the kitchen garden, the parks superintendent's house at Shrewsbury enjoyed the position and prospect of the big house itself. As a piece of landscape the Quarry owes a lot to the presence of the superb

Greek Revival church, St Chad's, which crowns its central and finest point on the northern edge. Looking to his left as he came out of the front door of Quarry Lodge Percy would see St Chad's just far enough away to be taken in as a whole. Turning right, to go into the Quarry or round to the glass-houses, he would look straight down the main lime avenue, pause on the boscage of the Dingle which broke the middle distance, then past it to the Severn, and finally up the sharp slope to Kingsland and Shrewsbury School.

Quarry Lodge itself was one of the Victorian embellishments of the park, a comfortable half-timbered villa with some of the black-and-white appearance which is the vernacular of Shropshire. Like the Quarry and the Dingle, the Lodge had had a bad war; when the Throwers took up residence the wartime decorations were well-worn but intact. It had been painted with materials left over from elsewhere and the walls, with their lower parts in dark green gloss, divided by a maroon stripe from the cream uppers, had a thoroughly institutional feel. It took a while to make the house more like home, and to make it a good place to bring up the children. Their eldest child, Margaret, had been born in 1944, and was followed by Susan in 1948, and Ann in 1952.

Here, especially during the show, Percy and Connie kept open house for their friends and, within reason, for other interested visitors too. Like her mother before her, Connie was called upon to entertain royalty, making the main bedroom available for Princess Alice, Countess of Athlone, to rest and powder her nose in during a visit to the show in 1957. Ann, then aged five, and a friend were in the room hidden, as they thought, under the bed. They were not missed by the Princess, who laughingly enquired as she came down the stairs: 'Whose are the tiny toes?'

The house came with the job and an annual salary of £300 with a cash allowance of £20 in lieu of fuel and light. Within three years these conditions were very considerably improved when Percy's department, which had previously been under the general purview of the borough surveyor, became a separate department directly accountable for itself.

The numbers of the staff, and the proportions of skilled and unskilled among them, fluctuated but averaged about thirty-five people, including at the outset two women. The presence of women on the staff was a peacetime novelty. Traditionally women had been considered either too weak or insufficiently clever for garden work. The necessities of the war changed that and so a few remained at Shrewsbury afterwards. It was not something that Percy thought necessary to consider, but when natural wastage took the women away their successors were men. Except as novelists, women have not been particularly conspicuous as creative artists. They have been comparatively prominent among gardeners, although usually as planters and carers rather than designers. At Sissinghurst, for example, Harold Nicolson was largely responsible for the design of the garden while his wife, Vita Sackville-West excelled at the planting stage. The same division of labour can be seen in innumerable gardens right down to the very humble. Percy's first major project at Shrewsbury was not at all women's work and was in any case largely done by outside contractors.

The felling and replanting of the lime avenues in the Quarry was to occupy Percy throughout his first five years at Shrewsbury. The useful, healthy life of a lime tree is usually around one hundred and fifty years. The earliest planted at Shrewsbury were thus sixty to seventy years beyond their normal life expectancy when Percy took over. They had been

71

planted very close together, so that all their growth had been forced upwards and they had not developed into natural shapes. Some were beginning to protest. Just before the war a small girl had been killed by a falling bough; there had been lesser injuries, and further disasters had been prevented only by emergency action. The people of Shrewsbury very naturally loved and cherished the trees, and while they might privately recognize that the trees had had their day they could not contemplate the idea of the Quarry without them, knowing that they would be unlikely to see their replacements in their maturity.

There is a place for ruthlessness in gardening, but Percy's action was necessary rather than ruthless. It made him mightily unpopular at all levels of town and county, which might have concerned him more than it did had he envisaged remaining at Shrewsbury instead of moving on to something bigger after four or five years as he and Connie planned. A few months after his arrival six limes were felled at the top of the main avenue. They revealed largely what Percy had expected and he had the trunks laid out to show the state of them to those who protested at the felling. The trunks were almost without exception hollow and rotten, with wasps' nests, mistletoe and all manner of fungi and parasites. Exact measurements were taken of the felled trees; the tallest was found to have been 133 feet high, or about one third over the average height of a normally mature lime.

The argument, won in principle, now turned into an argument about what exactly was going to replace the limes. Good arboricultural practice suggested that limes should not be planted again. Furthermore, the species of lime most often used for making avenues had certain disadvantages, notably a narcotic effect on bees, leading to abnormal and undesirable behaviour, and infestation by the Linden aphis, which caused them to drip and leave a sticky deposit. Fuelled by the intervention of the Lord Lieutenant of Shropshire, the Earl of Powis, and the wide-ranging fame of the lime avenues, the debate reached the correspondence columns of *The Times*.

It was perhaps Percy's once in a lifetime opportunity to follow in the footsteps of Capability Brown and to change and recreate a piece of landscape for several generations. Brown has his critics among practical gardeners: nobody can carp at one who was content to enjoy his creations only in his mind's eye, sacrificing for the sake of excellence and future generations any chance of actual enjoyment himself; but planting for an effect designed to be dramatic from a distance led, perhaps, to too much reliance on trees with heavy canopies and consequently greedy of the land around them. There were disputes as to which species should replace the limes. Leaving aside the question of species, Percy wanted to abandon the avenues and plant instead clumps of trees, with matching islands of flowering shrubs. This was a pattern of planting which he had known and loved since his days at Horwood. A start was made on putting the scheme into effect, helped by a few trees supplied from Sandringham by Charles Cook. A large island bed of rhododendrons was also planted, but this fell victim quite early on to the existing exigencies of access to the Flower Show. At the other extreme, Lord Powis started growing beech on his estate near Welshpool with a view to replanting the avenues with that species, and was still doing so in the spring of 1949 when the replanting programme was well under way.

Local feeling had had its way and the replacements were in the end limes, although planted much further apart than their predecessors so that each should make a specimen tree as well as contributing to the avenues. Tree planting can be a heart-breaking business; even in the most expert and loving hands a proportion of newly-planted trees will fail for no reason that can be explained, sometimes after they have been in for a couple of years and have shown every sign of being established and making good progress. Newly-planted trees are also irresistible to vandals, it seems. On one particularly good day Percy and his staff planted forty new limes in one of the avenues beside the Severn; the following morning, thirty-six of them had been broken off at shoulder level in what proved to have been the mindless outburst of a half-crazed youth with a boat-hook. Despite these setbacks the new limes were in place and generally established by the end of the 1952 planting season. Percy lived just long enough to see the avenues take their full majestic shape, with each of the trees mature except to the most practised and discerning eye. Provided limes are not stricken by some plague like the Dutch elm disease, the avenues in the Quarry will be at their best during the first half of the next century.

Progress on more short-term improvements suffered badly from the weather during Percy's early years at Shrewsbury. In 1946 and 1947 the Severn rose to nearly twenty feet above normal, flooding large areas of the town and causing havoc to some of the work in hand in the Quarry. Water backing-up filled the Dingle to the brim and undid most of the work that had been done towards its restoration. With all the heavy work in hand the soil in large parts of the Quarry was not fully compacted, which led to areas of it being left unstable. When the summer, particularly that of 1947, came and scorched the earth the dust rose and got into everything. The 1947 show was the first of the post-war era and had been delayed by a year partly to allow the new turf in the Quarry time to become established. This was just as well because on top of the flooding and scorching the Quarry was trodden by 120,000 people over the two days of the show.

The Quarry was not entirely suitable or adequate for the size of show that Shrewsbury had become. In addition, the town of Shrewsbury was in no sense built for motor traffic in any volume – and even today has not really come to terms with it. The very limited access to the Quarry was a nightmare in itself, and that was at the end of an impossibly congested route through narrow and tortuous streets. Nevertheless, the natural magnificence of the Quarry was sufficient justification for the trouble of getting there. These days, when the volume of motor traffic is of course much greater, visitors to the show have to park on certain specially appropriated sites away from the town centre and come in by means of a free bus shuttle.

At show time Shrewsbury was in its full plumage as a provincial capital. For the duration of the show it is also the capital of the entire British gardening world. Next to Chelsea it is this country's most important horticultural show and, with Southport, the last survivor of the once numerous major provincial shows. The others – Liverpool, Manchester, Sheffield, Leicester and Birmingham among them – have either disappeared or are much reduced versions of what they once were. In Percy's early years at Shrewsbury the show still had many characteristics of an old country fair, especially in the various acts which went on six hours a day on the open-air stage. Though latterly dominated by professional performers, some of these acts – weird, mimed allegories among them – would not have been out of place at a fair in a country town two hundred years ago. Interest in them waned rather as people became more accustomed to what the television had to offer. The musical element in the show continued throughout

Percy's years, however, and remains, especially the military bands and the singing by Welsh choirs.

Some of the regular judges at Shrewsbury, Charles Cook among them, were already well known to Percy; but others were no more than names on the schedule, and in due time became good and valued friends and colleagues, such as Roland Smith, head gardener to the Earl of Bradford at Weston-under-Lizard, and A. E. Fox at Hope Court, near Ludlow.

Judges at horticultural shows need more than an eye for an excellent, properly grown plant. They have to be prepared for attempted bribery and for personal dramas; for the streak of the prima donna which can lurk in the most staid and horny-handed of leek growers; for the bad blood, not just between individuals but of groups bound together by the contrasted loyalties of a dahlia or delphinium society or what ever. Gardeners may generally be good sorts, but the prospect of recognition and a prize can lead them into all manner of subterfuge, although this may perhaps be more common at the smaller and less formal shows without Shrewsbury's reputation. At the humbler level, anything has been known to be worth a try – the immersion of beetroot in blood to improve the colour, the artificial grafting of bunches of grapes to produce a seemingly gargantuan bunch, the replacement of damaged florets in cauliflowers by dropping in perfect ones from other plants, the concealment of cracks in carrots by filling them with carbolic soap, the imaginative use of wire and glue – all have been tried and for all anybody knows may here and there have passed a tired judge's eye.

The judges at the show did not like innovation of any kind. One change that was approved of over the years was the increase in the proportion of smaller or individual exhibitors.

In the early post-war years, the large seed firms – Suttons, Carters and the like – put on massive exhibits, up to sixty feet by twelve feet in size, but these became fewer. There was a general trend towards exhibiting smaller types of flowers and plants, sometimes those requiring dedicated attention over long periods, such as bonsais, and sometimes exotics such as the cacti in which Sir Oliver Leese, a pillar of the show and the Shropshire Horticultural Society, excelled. The Society had been a most generous patron of all gardening initiatives in the town. They could often be relied upon to step in when other resources failed or were exhausted.

Charles Cook was a valuable source of ideas and novelties. One of the stars of the 1948 Show had come originally from Sandringham: this was saintpaulia, the African violet, which is now one of the most reliable and even-tempered familiar house-plants but was then unknown to general gardeners. Although they require a certain amount of special care and a temperature, preferably even, around 60°F, they more than repay the trouble. They were exactly the sort of plant that Percy was later to bring to the enjoyment of millions.

Another even less demanding plant that Percy was to popularize hit Shrewsbury in a very big way in the late 1940s: fuchsias. Fuchsias had been about the houses and gardens of the sort in which Percy had spent much of his life but they were not, until the last thirty years or so, common in this country. Since then they have become very popular indeed and, in the pejorative sense, even vulgar. Their variety, peculiarity and flexibility are the qualities which make them popular now but it was their simple oddity which attracted botanists in the first place. James Lee, a very successful commercial nurseryman at Hammersmith (and a considerable botanist in his own right) was informed of one on a window ledge in Wapping in the 1750s and hastened over there to look at it. The plant was in the house of a woman who said that her husband had brought it back with him from the West Indies and she was not inclined to sell it at any price. It was literally only all the money that Lee had in his pockets that induced her to change her mind. From Lee the species spread rapidly through his network of discerning and often eminent customers.

Percy's discovery of a stock of very old fuchsia plants was the brightest point of his first day as superintendent at Shrewsbury. At the time of his arrival there were only three glasshouses in the Quarry. Under the fuel restrictions in force in 1946, glasshouses could only be heated if seventy-five per cent of their area was used for growing food crops. Within these restrictions Percy immediately began to build up from the fifty or so existing fuchsia plants, taking tips and then further tips as soon as the first generation was rooted, and so on. By the end of May, when conditions were ready for planting out to begin, the stock had grown to more than five thousand. It was a considerable achievement, even allowing for the reliability and good temper of the species, and to Percy the economy with which it had been done was a satisfying contrast to the prodigality and waste which seems to have caused him real disquiet at Leeds and elsewhere in the municipal gardening world.

Shrewsbury became, and remains, famous for its fuchsias. In time more than one hundred varieties were to thrive in the Dingle alone; but they were also prominent in the schemes of floral decoration around the town, where they were displayed in every possible style from standards to pendulous. The co-operation of the shop and hotel keepers in the town was encouraged by organizing competitions among them.

Apart from the replanting of the Dingle, Percy was involved in the making of a particularly imaginative garden overseas. This was in Berlin where, at the beginning of 1951, it was felt that a sufficient spirit of new friendship had grown up between the British and the people of Berlin to warrant a peaceful, lasting memorial. The idea that this should take the form of a garden seems to have been originated by Berlin's superintendent of parks, a man called Witte, who had been enthralled by English gardens, especially their turf, when visiting the Festival of Britain. The idea was passed to the General Officer Commanding the British Sector of Berlin, Major-General G. K. Bourne, who by reason of personal connections went to E. P. Everest, then chairman of the Shropshire Horticultural Society, for advice. In his capacity of honorary horticultural adviser to the Society, as well as parks superintendent, Percy was dispatched to Berlin to reconnoitre.

It was the first time he had ever left his country and, following his experiences on aircraft during the journeys rather hoped he would not have to do so again. The flight out was from Northolt. They took off in a thunderstorm. The first thing Percy saw when he had steeled himself to look out of the window was a small nut on the aircraft's wing jigging violently up and down. 'I did not,' he later recalled, 'take my eyes off that nut until we were on the ground in Berlin and the engines had been turned off.' The return journey was worse. The aircraft was discernibly decrepit, even to Percy's inexpert eye. He well remembered the stewardess remarking to him in the casual manner of a seasoned traveller: 'This one won't be as comfortable . . . there's a strike at Northolt, so we've got to use this old Dakota.' Though the most reliable of aircraft in the longer term, Dakotas had got off to a bad start, and as the jigging nut had made his outward journey seem apocalyptic, so the ghoulish folklore surrounding Dakotas infested Percy's mind all the way back.

Fortunately Herr Witte, Percy's counterpart in Berlin, had excellent English, and the two got on very well both personally and professionally. Witte later came over and stayed at Quarry Lodge for a few weeks which included the Shrewsbury Show. From that and from visits to other gardens in England under Percy's guidance he returned to nurture the Berlin garden with a thoroughly Anglicized hand. Witte's daughter, Ursula, a near contemporary of Margaret Thrower, also stayed at Quarry Lodge for some months a few years later in the course of improving her English.

The land on which it was proposed to make the English Garden in Berlin was in the Tiergarten, which was the first piece of land in a European city made available for the public to walk in. The land was naturally boggy and as such not entirely suitable for its public purposes. Nevertheless, it was tamed, improved and well planted over the years, and by the eve of the Second World War extended to some eight hundred acres, whose cultured beauty fully justified their international fame. The war had undone most of it; the few trees that remained after shelling and bombing had, in desperation, been cut down and used for fuel. In this wilderness Percy and Witte marked out an area of six acres, drew rough plans and agreed planting schemes in principle. Although the garden was to be a joint enterprise, the bulk of the trees, plants and shrubs were to come from England and Percy returned to set about their procurement.

The plans were exhibited at the 1951 Shrewsbury Show and an appeal made to the members and exhibitors for contributions. Despite the pacific atmosphere in which the garden was being made the President of the Society, Lieutenant-General Sir Oliver Leese, had some comfortable words for any doubters:

Remember that when you are dealing with Germans you are dealing with people very different from ourselves. A German will do very fine things if led by the right man. I often wonder why we do not send a leader over there.

Thoughtful and generous offers came very willingly from the Society's members; and also more substantial stocks from the growers. Gregorys and Wheatcrofts between them provided all that any English gardener could wish for in roses, and Carters and Suttons were generous with the grass seed that Witte coveted. Individual gardeners beyond the immediate reach of Shrewsbury were also approached. King George VI instructed Eric Savill to assist with the many appropriate species which flourished in his garden. The Savill Garden at Windsor had been just a bog garden in the days when Percy had observed its beginnings from a distance, and bog and waterside plants happened to be Eric Savill's abiding speciality. In addition to a stock of these, the Berlin garden was privileged to be given, through the Savill Garden, one of only three metasequoias then growing in Britain. The first specimens had been found in Central China during the war; in 1945 they were pronounced to be living relics of a fossil genus.

Witte evidently absorbed the spirit of English gardening fully and quickly. In planting-up the English Garden in Berlin he excavated a lake from the sodden ground to help drain the surrounding area on which he established flower and shrub borders, around a framework of trees and large specimen shrubs, underplanted with drifts of naturalized spring bulbs, all set in close-cut, well-watered turf. As well as a tribute to the new spirit of friendship, Anthony Eden, then Foreign Secretary, suggested in his speech at the opening of the garden in May 1952, that it was English enough to give 'a sweet nostalgic pleasure to the staff of a new British Embassy'.

Percy himself, though not given to nostalgia or any show of sentiment, never spent a night away from home if it could possibly be avoided. From the early 1950s, however, he was to see less and less of home, and indeed of Shrewsbury, during his waking hours.

6

Gardening on Radio and Television

Within two or three years of his arrival at Shrewsbury Percy had made enough of an impact on the town for it to be clear that he was no ordinary parks superintendent. Although the requirements of his job and the need to make a reliable living always took precedence in his mind over everything else, the possibility of following and developing his career through different channels existed from the early 1950s. In the event, the only casualty from this state of affairs was that he abandoned any plans to move from Shrewsbury after a few years to some larger town, and remained in his post until he reached the normal retirement age in 1974.

There came a time when the authorities at Shrewsbury well understood and appreciated the advantages of having a national figure in their employment; but in the early years they did not always approve of Percy's absences and were not particularly generous in their responses to his requests for leave of absence on semi-official business. As late as 1955 – a year in which Percy was surprised to read of himself described as a 'veteran broadcaster' – he was given permission to be absent to attend only one of the four days of the Chelsea Flower Show.

He filled his job to an unusual degree, however. Throughout his time as superintendent he never had more than one secretary; outside, he was customarily so ubiquitous with advice, verbal and practical, warning, prodding, demonstrating and lending a hand, that his actual presence was missed even during the dullest of mid-winter routines.

Percy learnt to garden by the immemorial means of watching and then doing likewise. This peerless but very leisurely way of learning was becoming extinct, together with the types of garden in which it had been practised – the comfortable private estates where Percy himself had spent his formative years. At Leeds he had seen the back-to-back dwellers who, unless they were allotment keepers, had no opportunity at all to garden. At Derby, in the 'Dig for Victory' effort, he had been surprised at how eagerly many of the previously idle or uninitiated took to gardening with enthusiasm. Then, next to the intangible question of patriotism, the people had been moved by the need to eat. That need for self-sufficiency had gone within five or six years of the end of the war, but there remained the pleasure and satisfaction, not to mention apparent economy, of providing for oneself. Beyond this there was the vast area of the domestic pleasure garden to be explored for a new generation. Percy had seen and foreseen all this, though he had never articulated it; and in doing so he was very lucky in being where he was when he was.

Some area of garden had been an essential feature of the Victorian suburbs. The far larger suburbs made up by the endless developments of semi-detached houses between the two World Wars were designed even more to tempt the abeyant gardener within all Englishmen. The ancient Chinese would have approved: they believed – and practised the ideal – that a garden was essential to civilized life. It had to be private, and provide an opportunity for men to return to the rhythms of nature, and to exercise the senses of sight, smell and hearing. What could be more agreeable? Or indeed more practicable? Taken on the literal Chinese model, the entire population of the British Isles, it has been calculated, could be housed with a garden within a radius of thirty-five miles of Little Horwood. Alas, the British, unlike the ancient Chinese, need space, or at least room to be more than an arm's length from their neighbour. As sources of acrimony and litigation, boundaries, garden fences and unneighbourly behaviour leave even divorce far behind.

The garden of a typical inter-war semi-detached house, though generous in size by modern standards, usually had certain built-in problems. The nature of the layout created wind tunnels and, as finished by the contractor, the owner of the prospective garden would usually be left confronting his neighbours on two or possibly three sides, divided from them by a flimsy partition, probably no more than waist high. The problems of turning such sites into fragments of paradise had, however, been submerged by the emergencies of war by the time Percy began to tread the stage as a teacher of gardening, rather than as a practitioner only.

He did not at first relish public speaking. One of his earliest talks was to a Townswomen's Guild at Derby and the prospect of addressing them so alarmed him that he was careful to arrive at the meeting just sufficiently primed with whisky. The technique required for a 'Dig for Victory' demonstration came to him more naturally. Here the crisp, almost barked style of instruction, followed by a question-and-answer session, was redolent of the slightly military way of receiving and giving instructions in the Royal Gardens at Windsor.

Young gardeners were not put before their 'Dig for Victory' audiences entirely untutored. They were given some basic instruction by those already practised at teaching gardening by word as much as by example. In Percy's case, he was sent to the Boots Company's Research Station at Lenton, near

85

Nottingham, to listen to Arthur Billitt. Arthur Billitt was as much a scientist and theorist as a practical gardener. He was the sort of gardener whom Percy had certainly never heard talk before. When Arthur came over to Derby to do a series of lectures in the area, Percy made time to follow him around. Percy had listened to a few theorists and worked with many practitioners. Arthur Billitt was one of a then rare breed, an experimental gardener by occupation, in touch with all relevant scientific developments, and a fanatically hard-working gardener in his leisure time. The voice of gardening, in the broadcast sense, before the war had been C. H. Middleton, who was described as the 'best-known gardener since Adam'. In 1938 Middleton took a six-week holiday and suggested that Arthur might fill his place during that time. The BBC scrutinized Arthur and decided that he was not acceptable because of his position with Boots. Middleton thought again and this time suggested Fred Streeter, who was to become the most familiar gardening voice on BBC Radio.

Broadcast gardening came surprisingly late to the BBC – surprisingly because the wholesome flavour of self-improvement that goes with the garden might have been thought to be close to the missionary spirit of Lord Reith. Early programmes were occasionally interspersed with all manner of tit-bits of topical information, and seasonal jobs in the garden found a place among them; gardening programmes as such were given mainly to talks on fairly specialized subjects. The founding fathers of the BBC were, at least, entirely open to suggestions and contributions, including ones from people they had never previously heard of. Each broadcast was to some extent an experiment or an exploration.

The very first gardening broadcast was on roses in the summer of 1923. Charles Unwin, the Cambridgeshire seeds-

man, called on the person who was to make it, and was
advised to drop in at Savoy Hill and suggest doing a similar
item on sweet peas. Unwin duly called at Savoy Hill and, in a
small office, was promptly interviewed by one who, for want
of anyone else, turned out to be the head of London broadcasting. The first and perfectly reasonable question was:
'What do you know about sweet peas?' Unwin explained
himself and his connection with his celebrated family firm but
was stopped by his interlocutor with the exclamation, 'Good-
ness me, I'm one of your customers!' Unwin duly proceeded
to give what proved to be the first of thousands of broadcasts
spread over thirty-eight years.

Early broadcasters had to be men of all work. While
touching-up his script just before a broadcast, Unwin was
approached by an announcer with a problem. 'Lloyd George,'
he said, 'has just been made a chief by a tribe of Red Indians
which spells its name S-I-O-U-X. Do you know how you
pronounce it?' This was before the age of Westerns, when the
'Sooh' entered common usage, and after various trials Unwin
could only suggest that it must be 'Seex', and thus it was
broadcast.

Meanwhile, the BBC's diet of gardening tit-bits grew into
one of 'bulletins', which it broadcast on every issue that could
possibly be of public concern or interest. Gradually the then
editor of the Royal Horticultural Society's *Journal*, F. J. Chit-
tenden, established what was in effect a series of gardening
bulletins.

There was still no sound of the 'personality', the bane or the
blessing of modern broadcasting, depending on one's point of
view, although with very few exceptions most of the stars of
broadcast gardening have been as wholesome and acceptable
as their subject matter. The first to become a regular feature,

recognizable for himself, was C. H. Middleton, who was recommended to the BBC by the Royal Horticultural Society in response to the corporation's request for somebody suitable to broadcast. Middleton's career was not so remote from the course that Percy's might have followed, except that Percy was discovered by the BBC in his early thirties, while Middleton had been ten years older and well-established in a different arm of the gardening profession by the time he arrived at the BBC.

His father had been a head gardener at Weston-under-Weedon in Northamptonshire, not far from Horwood. Although he stayed at school until he was seventeen, he too had worked as a gardener in private service. Unlike Percy, his evenings during late adolescence seem to have been spent over his books because he became enough of a botanist to work for a while at Kew. During the First World War he was engaged in making the people dig for victory, and after the war he became a civil servant, first as a Ministry of Agriculture Inspector, and later as an instructor in horticulture with the Surrey County Council. At the BBC his fortnightly series *The Week in the Garden* became from 1934 the weekly *In Your Garden*, which by the end of the war had an estimated audience of three and a half million. But for his early death at the age of fifty-seven in 1945, the BBC might not have been in need of a new gardening voice for another ten years and Percy's opportunity might have passed.

Middleton had all the qualities that were to make Percy a natural and successful broadcaster in his field. First, his expertise was unanswerable, although it was exercised with quiet modesty. 'You know,' Percy was fond of saying, 'if you pick up a plant, it will tell you what it needs. . . . You've got to care about your plants . . . spend time on them.' Second, like

Percy, he loved his subject with the passion which only those whose work is their hobby can know, and this was manifest in their voices and, in Percy's case, gestures, as they communicated their feeling to millions.

Towards the end of the war the BBC, knowing how the 'Dig for Victory' effort had fuelled interest in gardening, started to plan how to carry on afterwards. In 1947 a producer in Manchester, Robert Stead, decided to tap the nation's enthusiasm for gardening with a new question-and-answer programme, *How Does Your Garden Grow?* The first broadcast came from an hotel in Ashton-under-Lyne in April 1947, with two nervous gardeners – Fred Loads of Lancaster and Bill Sowerbutts of Ashton-under-Lyne – on the platform and Stead in the chair. The broadcast was not without incident. An eighty-one-year-old man in the audience thought he was taking part in the programme 'Have a Go' and insisted on playing his cornet. Loads and Sowerbutts, an endearingly quarrelsome pair, were joined on the team in 1950 by Alan Gemmell of Keele University to form the long-serving team of the legendary programme *Gardeners' Question Time*. The programme was originally regional and before it reached the national network had imitators on other regions, in some of which Percy participated. His real introduction to broadcasting, however, came in the finest tradition of broadcast gardening, by accident.

One afternoon in the autumn of 1948 Godfrey Baseley – one of the greater figures in British broadcasting and the begetter, among much else, of *The Archers* – was passing a few idle moments in Shrewsbury by walking in the Dingle. On his way out of the Quarry he poked his head round Percy's office door, introduced himself and asked: 'Who's in charge of that garden?' Baseley at the time was doing a programme called

Beyond the Back Door, a series very much in the 'Dig for Victory' spirit, with items on every productive pursuit to which a backyard could be turned. In peace, the pleasure garden was beckoning, and the programme's role was to take the spirit of 'Dig for Victory' into the era of 'Dig for Plenty'. Baseley invited Percy to contribute about ten minutes to the programme and, largely in ignorance of what was involved, Percy agreed to make himself available the following Sunday afternoon.

Being the early autumn it was decided to make Percy's contribution about the planting of some shrubs and he collected a few together by a border near one of the Quarry greenhouses ready for the arrival of Baseley and Leonard Clift, a slightly more practised broadcasting hand who was also to take part. It was not until the session was over that Baseley told Percy it was in fact a live broadcast. Even so, Percy could eat neither breakfast nor luncheon on the great day and this broadcast might surprise those familiar with Percy's broadcasting style in later years. Baseley addressed Percy as 'Mr Thrower' throughout; Leonard Clift, the old hand, was addressed as 'Clift'. The broadcast seems to have gone something like this:

> Baseley: What's this then?
> Percy: Er . . . I've forgotten its name at present . . . it's suitable for rockeries . . . I think.
> Clift: (Inaudible)
> Percy: Er . . . yes . . . yes . . . that's it. It's one of those.
> Baseley: What?
> Clift: (Inaudible)
> Baseley: I see. . . . Right. . . . What's this then?

– and so on.

Back in Birmingham the broadcast was recorded. Although this first performance lacked what might be called fluency and polish, something in Percy's whole deportment in relation to his subject and the microphone rang an encouraging bell in Baseley's mind. He telephoned Percy and, making imaginative use of the truth, told him the broadcast was 'first rate' and asked whether he would come into Birmingham at some point to try a ten-minute broadcast from a script. The script, on what to do in the garden during the coming month, was written and approved, and in due course Percy presented himself at the studios in Birmingham to read it. Seated in the studio, face to face with the microphone, Percy was not at all happy. His stomach churned and his hands shook; indeed they shook so much that the rustling of his script would be picked up by the microphone. He thought he might manage better if he stood up and asked the studio manager, Tony Shryane, who was also a distinguished and long-lasting editor of *The Archers*, whether he could do so. 'Nobody ever stands up in a studio to do a recording,' said Shryane firmly. The reason for this was that a standing position tended to produce rather a hollow sound in the acoustic techniques of the time. Nevertheless Percy insisted, and stood, his script placed on an improvised lectern. Thereafter he stood whenever possible throughout his long broadcasting career. At this first recording he was not only suffering the surprise of hearing his own voice, but the knowledge that hundreds of thousands of other people would be hearing it too.

While this period of stage fright passed soon enough, he was never entirely at ease with a prepared script and before very long gave up using one. Like any good performer he never ceased to suffer from nerves, although in later years he would be vastly more nervous reading the lesson in church

91

than in front of a camera. He was essentially rather a shy man; but his absolute commitment to and familiarity with the subject overcame what could have been a disability. It was also the quality that Baseley recognized in him and which put him in the Middleton tradition. It was perhaps shown at its best in what amounted to informal question-and-answer sessions, a style that successive producers employed with enormous skill, often in subtle or indiscernible ways.

With these basic strengths, Percy's broadcasting style did not need to be embroidered. Some of the voices of gardening have been little short of caricatures. Percy, however, did not need such props as a loamy accent or earthy catch-phrases. If he had an idiosyncrasy it was in repeating himself, or at least in repeating the name of a plant under discussion, somewhat in the manner of a good-tempered sergeant-major giving instructions.

As all Percy's classic performances were unscripted they cannot be readily recreated in print. But his voice can be heard through the following example, especially if one imagines his hands probing and caressing the rose to show the extent and whereabouts of the mildew, pausing no doubt here and there to use a spray or one of the other gadgets he loved:

Mildew is one of the commonest diseases affecting rose foliage. It is seen as white powdery or mealy patches on leaves, stems and buds. It thrives in a damp atmosphere and so is most prevalent in a wet season or in gardens that have a poor circulation of air. In severe or prolonged attacks plants may be weakened and shoots and buds crippled. . . . It is almost impossible to eliminate mildew entirely. . . . Spraying with copper or other fungicide is a useful control. It is most easily controlled by preventive sprays before the disease has appeared. Four or five sprays during June, July and August will usually ensure a reasonable degree of freedom [from] mildew.

Percy's voice never caused the engineers problems with 'level'. Although his accent was hard, his voice was resonant and his utterances properly enunciated in the manner of one brought-up to speak and be spoken to politely and clearly. His accent itself is a mystery. Percy used to describe it as a 'mongrel' accent. There was much of rural Buckinghamshire in it. The accent of that region, now very seldom heard at all, is one of this country's less attractive tones of voice. But the very short 'A's of Percy's speech did not come from Buckinghamshire, and it seems unlikely that he could have acquired them during his few years in Yorkshire.

Such was the raw material – raw, that is to say, in relation to the broadcasting media – with which Godfrey Baseley and his successors had to work. Percy became a regular contributor to *Beyond the Back Door* with a monthly item on what to attend to in the garden. A little later, this was extended to a second regular spot in which the programme visited a famous or peculiar garden and talked to its owner or keeper. This was the sort of broadcast at which Percy excelled, whether talking to a specialist grower or to those such as A. E. Fox or Roland Smith who were great funds of gardening wisdom. One or two of the owners of the grander houses visited by the programme were put out by the associations of the title *Beyond the Back Door* and so its name was changed to the relatively classless *In Your Garden*.

Percy's first appearance on television came in 1951 when the programme *Picture Page* broadcast an item on the English Garden in Berlin. The producer on that occasion was Barrie

Edgar. Barrie Edgar was Percy's first gardening producer on television and, as things turned out, came back in the same role during his last years on *Gardeners' World*. The other producers were David Attenborough (then very much in the emergent phase), Kenneth Milne-Buckley, John Furness (who, with Godfrey Baseley, did much to give Percy a nationally-networked programme), John Farringdon, Paul Morby (with whom the all-important transfer from black and white to colour was planned), Bill Duncalf, and then Barrie Edgar again.

The first television series with which Percy was associated, *Country Calendar*, was usually presented by Godfrey Baseley with Barrie Edgar producing. *Country Calendar* used outside locations, very often the grounds of the Staffordshire Farm Institute at Penkridge, near Cannock, or Church End Farm at Maxstoke between Coventry and Birmingham. It discussed all manner of country pursuits and crafts – shooting, thatching, angling, walking, cycling, wheelwrighting – with Percy's regular contributions covering timely garden jobs at their due seasons. The BBC had been looking for a location like Church End Farm. The farmhouse was a good-looking brick building, typical of the area, and it was the centre of a working farm, owned by the Gold family who sometimes took part in the programmes. Certain changes, including the laying of a concrete path to carry cameras, made it ideal for television. It was, furthermore, in direct line with the BBC's transmitter at Sutton Coldfield.

The successor to *Country Calendar* in Percy's television career was *Out and About*. The programme was an innovation in at least two respects. First, it had one linkman in London, who introduced and explained the various activities which different parts of the programme covered. Second, it was broadcast on a Sunday afternoon and was the first such programme to appear at that time. As it happened, one of Percy's contributions happened to be first on the programme on its first afternoon and so he has the exact if minor distinction of being the first person to address the nation over the television on a Sunday afternoon.

Television is exceedingly greedy. With the possible exception of the spoken word nothing can consume, absorb and exhaust the interest of a scene or subject in a shorter time. A measured television sweep of a garden can, in skilled hands, not only encapsulate the garden but reveal a remarkable amount of detail too. What is entrancing at the first look can be fully explained at the second, and thereafter too easily become repetitive. The *Country Calendar* formula thus had its limitations. What was needed in addition to an established garden to be viewed, discussed, replanned and replanted as part of the regular schedule, was a garden so infinite in its variety and capable of such sudden change as previously unknown to nature. Such a garden was to be the hallmark of the programme *Gardening Club,* which, with an audience of three million, saw the emergence of gardening into the first division in British television.

The site of the television garden was at Gosta Green, in a converted cinema and wrestling arena not far from the truly dreadful centre of Birmingham. The studio had many uses apart from *Gardening Club* and the garden had to be to some extent recreated every week, when rather more than a ton of topsoil was trundled into Birmingham to lay the foundations of what was undoubtedly the best-known garden in Britain. The two greenhouses and a lean-to garden shed were made to be erected in rather less than half an hour and when folded up were amazingly compact to store. The greenhouses had no

95

glass in them, to avoid reflections and to enable the cameras to move very close to the plant under discussion. Godfrey Baseley had told Percy to practise some of the more delicate garden operations that were customarily shown close up in a mirror, so that his audience could more easily remember and follow his example.

The glassless glasshouses had to be taken very seriously. Percy lapsed once or twice, including an occasion when, on camera, he found the greenhouse door stuck and, without thinking, put his hand through where the glass supposedly was and opened the door from within. There was a supply of other props to hand to make a garden for any season of any type, including ten tons of stones for rock-gardens. There was also a hot line to a supply of goldfish should a pond be called for. The whole was completed by a backdrop of wattle fencing, awaiting Percy's arrival for the planting up with a collection of plants from Shrewsbury in his car.

The transport of these plants for use and demonstration on programmes had been a minor bone of contention between Percy and the BBC during the earlier years. The BBC's accounts people would countenance a third-class rail fare and a night's subsistence; nothing more. Thus, when he was called to London or beyond from Shrewsbury he was obliged by the railway timetables of the early 1950s to stay away from home for the night, which was something he hated having to do. When he started carrying supplies of plants with him he asked for expenses to cover travel by car instead and was told that the BBC would cover the cost of their transport separately but would still not countenance the use of the car. Percy was not an avaricious man but neither was he in any position to subsidize the BBC.

It was on evenings marooned in London that he quite often

visited casinos, as gambling was one of the few things which he had an inclination for when on his own. Once he had induced the BBC to pay his travelling costs by road life was a great deal more flexible. Increasingly, of course, he had friends with whom to stay in London. He would arrive at John Furness's house at Barnes, for example, with his car crammed with fruit and vegetables and other materials left over from a broadcast. His visits were much enjoyed by the Furness children and he in turn delighted in their company as indeed he did that of all children. He would have dearly loved to have a son of his own. In the mornings he would arrange his time of departure to coincide with that of the children to school, so that he could take them there usually leaving them with a ten shilling note.

With the freedom of travelling by road he could also arrange an hospitable port of call between London and Shrewsbury for an overnight stay, such as his mother's house at Little Horwood. Old Mrs Thrower was a widow for thirty-five years, until her death in 1974. For much of that time she kept a shop at Little Horwood and only succumbed to age and retirement when decimalization came in.

Gardening Club continued until the arrival of colour television. In few other fields of television was the development of colour as important as in gardening. Much excellent practical work could be done and demonstrated in black and white but the real impact of gardening on television needed colour; through it the viewers could establish an extraordinary intimacy with the plants and the presenters did not have to spend probably ineffectual time trying to describe the finer points of colour. Details and characteristics previously unknown to the layman could be pin-pointed and explained by an expert hand. It led to a rise in expectations of what could be done and of standards that could be achieved in almost any garden. These rising standards themselves presented further challenges to gardening producers and presenters: in colour the *Gardening Club* studio garden was more difficult to present convincingly and it was thus time to move outside again.

Percy always dressed in the same way when on television. It happened to be the way he always dressed. He knew how a head gardener should dress for a routine day and dressed accordingly. His green or brown jacket and trousers might not always match but when they did they could be described as a suit. He always wore a tie. It became part of the routine of *Gardening Club* broadcasts from Gosta Green for him to go into the glassless glasshouse, take off his jacket and hang it on the back of the door, and then roll up his shirt sleeves while introducing the day's topic. These preliminaries in the glass-house became in a way his trademark. On one occasion the ritual came to a halt three times, when the jacket fell from its hook to the floor. The floor crew, who were fond of practical jokes, had substituted a collapsible hook on the door. Percy's professionalism was stretched to keep a straight face as he laid the jacket aside and proceeded to talk.

Patience and a straight face were frequently required, par-ticularly with some of the specialists previously unfamiliar with television as performers who came in to take part in programmes. Nervous beginners tended to talk too much, or to make a terrible mess of demonstrating what they habitually did brilliantly, like the lady flower arranger who reduced her supply of flowers to pulp during rehearsals. Percy's job on these occasions was to soothe or encourage contributors to try again, although he often ended up doing the job himself.

Percy generally did most of the talking on any programme.

Lord Aberconway, later President of the Royal Horticultural Society, recalls that he first met him in 1952:

> I was asked to appear with Francis Hanger, the curator of the RHS garden at Wisley, on Percy's weekly programme to discuss rhododendrons. For this, I had to have a pancake mix put on my hands and face, I remember, to keep them from shining. The show was then in monochrome so Hanger and I in our dialogue kept having to refer to 'this red' or 'this yellow' rhododendron. Apparently we were so successful in our discussion that Percy let us use up almost all of his hour and he himself talked on geraniums, I recall, for only five minutes, an unprecedented situation I afterwards learnt.

Lord Aberconway's garden at Bodnant in North Wales was one of the places covered in the visits to celebrated gardens which were one of the happiest developments of gardening on television. What could be more agreeable than to be shown round a great garden by the owner and Percy, usually with the resident head gardener and others available to answer questions? The Countess of Rosse's garden at Nymans in Sussex was one of several which were so successful on television that programmes from them became regular features.

Some garden owners took more easily than others to appearing on television. Percy and John Furness once went to record a programme at the Dowager Marchioness of Londonderry's garden at Mount Stewart in County Down. Lady Londonderry, nicknamed the 'Duchess of Ulster', was then near the end of a glittering life. In her day she had been known to appear at the State Opening of Parliament to all appearances clothed entirely in diamonds; a serpent tattooed round one of her ankles suggested where her other interests lay. Percy and Furness arrived at Mount Stewart the day before the scheduled recording to discuss ideas for the programme with Lady Londonderry and her head gardener, Bolus. After a long wait at the door, it was opened by a sleepy and dishevelled footman, and it was clear they were in for a very Irish experience. The large party at luncheon were of all ages and conditions, but all members or various kinsmen of the Vane-Tempest-Stewart family. Percy and Furness emerged from the dining room rippling with suppressed laughter, into the gardens which were an anti-climax by comparison. To Furness it was 'just a rich woman's garden', but despite Lady Londonderry's undoubted enthusiasm and Bolus's hard work it had gone rather down hill. The gardens were in many parts. There was a 'Dodo Walk', lined with concrete beasts untraceable to the dawn of history; there was a 'Red Hand of Ulster Garden', planned to be full of heraldic topiary, where most of the yew had long gone its own way.

After a lifetime in the limelight Lady Londonderry was highly excited by the idea of appearing on television. When Percy and the whole team arrived at Mount Stewart the following morning she was ready and keen to get on. It was customary on these occasions for Percy to introduce the setting and then proceed to draw the owner into the programme. Lady Londonderry was positioned on the terrace for Percy to talk his way towards her until the point came for her to join in when she was asked to say 'Good morning, Mr Thrower'. She was aghast at the idea of addressing a gardener as 'Mister'. Bolus was Bolus, Percy must be 'Thrower'. Percy, who had addressed her as 'My Lady' throughout, did not mind what she called him, but Furness felt that people who saw the programme regularly might think it was a bit odd. Lady

Londonderry conceded that point. Once into the unscripted no-man's-land of the programme proper, however, she set sail to take over. Guided by a gesticulating Furness, Percy in effect backed Lady Londonderry off camera into the care of one of the crew and the programme took its course. It was not the last of Lady Londonderry. Like a naughty child aware that she had gone too far, she popped up wordlessly from time to time, from behind a shrub or over a hedge. The eventual programme was a memorable one. Nobody was offended. Although pre-recorded, there were no re-takes and very little editing.

Much of *Gardening Club* had been staged outside the studio, whether on visits to famous gardens or to almost anywhere when the time came to demonstrate proper hedge cutting or the pruning of roses. Visitors to the Quarry and the Dingle at Shrewsbury became accustomed to seeing the roses half pruned or perhaps a hedge half trimmed, awaiting the cameras for whose benefit the jobs would be completed. When, with colour, the programme became *Gardeners' World*, the plan was to make a garden of the BBC's own, and one was duly begun on an allotment next to the Botanic Garden in Birmingham. One allotment measuring thirty yards by ten yards may or may not have been practicable to maintain to an acceptable standard; but soon Paul Morby, the producer, enlarged the holding to cover six allotments. Such an area soon enough fell victim to nature and a lack of daily care on the considerable scale required. The standard was short of what the ever more fastidious viewers had come to expect and complaints began to figure in the four hundred or so letters a week which each programme brought it. The answer seemed to be in the making of a garden specially for television, a real garden of a realistic size kept up to standard by a proud owner.

101

It is a remarkable fact that although Percy was now quite commonly known as 'Britain's head gardener' he had never in his life really had a garden of his own, let alone of his own creation. No garden that has not been started from something prior to scratch can properly be called one's own. Percy's opportunity to make such a garden of his own came, like so much else in his fortunate life, by chance.

7

The Magnolias

During the years when he took root in Shropshire many of Percy's friends were made among the people with whom he spent the odd day shooting. The shoots spilled over into the evenings for supper, when the women joined them, and thereafter very often into interminable games of cards on which the farmers, who made up many of Percy's and Connie's friends, were very keen. Perhaps Percy's closest friends were John and Doug Whittingham. The latter in due time became his accountant, while John ran the family farm some miles north of Shrewsbury, adjacent to country over which they often shot. Towards the end of the 1950s the farmer on the land next to the Whittinghams went bankrupt. John Whittingham was inclined to buy part of it but not the whole because it was not good farming land. In the event Percy and Doug Whittingham together bought the surplus land; they improved it a little by levelling it off and growing a crop or so of barley before returning it to grass, while continuing to shoot over it. It was during one of the shoots that Percy paused and looked at the view, a prospect of sixty miles, taking in a vast tract of the rich Shropshire landscape, with the legendary hills – the Wrekin, Wenlock Edge, Caer Caredoc, the Stiperstones and the Long Mynd – mysteriously resplendent in it. No imagination was required to see the spot as a superb site for a house.

Connie could not at first see the point of all the trouble and expense that would be involved in building a house on the

103

site. They had, after all, a perfectly adequate house which went with the job. Percy, however, was not far off being a mere ten years from retirement, when they would certainly need somewhere to live; and that fact, underlined by Percy's unspoken determination to go ahead, settled the matter.

The house, a four-bedroomed chalet bungalow, was not pretentious. It could have come from any builder's catalogue of basic designs. Percy and Connie wanted the house built towards the top of the sloping site to make the very most of the prospect, and to have the principal rooms along the south side of the house overlooking the garden. Otherwise all they required were a sound building and basic comfort, both of which were assured by the local contractor who built the house. Anything exceptional about the establishment awaited the garden, on which Percy planned to make a serious start during the winter of 1963.

Apart from the splendours which in due time grew up outside, there was relatively little about the actual house at The Magnolias to suggest that a gardener lived there. The professional side of the owner was largely confined to the hall, with its collection of prizes and trophies, although Percy shared some of this space with Charles Cook. Beyond the hall the house was made solely for comfortable living, and for entertaining the large numbers of people – friends, gardening experts, film crews – who passed through the house on nine days out of ten. Providing for them, on top of looking after Percy and the girls, kept Connie more than fully occupied. She had a full share in the planning of the garden, as she had that of the house, both when it was on paper and as it began to take shape. Her judgments were often formed more quickly than Percy's in deciding whether a particular shrub was wrongly – or could be better – sited, and quicker to insist on a change.

The site was difficult. It was six hundred feet above sea level and on a slope sharp enough to be noticeable when walking on it. The soil was gravelly around the house itself, with a strand of medium loam along towards the front gate, and heavy clay at the bottom of the slope which was inclined to become waterlogged. At about an acre and a half the garden was big enough to take some serious trees and those Percy planted included a cedar of Lebanon and a blue cedar. Otherwise, for all that he was 'Britain's head gardener', Percy found himself to a surprising extent confronted by the new in setting about the design of the garden. The name of the house – The Magnolias – had been the result of a request for suggestions from readers of *Amateur Gardening*; other suggestions had included 'Thrower's Patch' and the like. In many ways the garden, too, was much of the sort that a reader of *Amateur Gardening* might have made for himself given the time, the resources and, most of all, the energy. Most fashionable garden designers of the present would probably regard the garden of The Magnolias as a chamber of horrors, full of assaults on the senses and breaches of taste. That must be a matter of opinion. The fact is that the garden was made very much as a plantsman's garden, that it was exceedingly well done and that it must be delectable to live with.

Percy allowed himself eight years to bring the garden to a basic maturity. He did not get off to a good start because the first winter, 1963, was one of the worst of the century and little progress could be made. The basic design was to be informal because the site, somewhat in the manner of a vineyard, would be visible from some way around and any emphasis on straight lines would not consort well with the native landscape. Tradition was followed with the pleached hawthorn hedging on the east and north boundaries, and the wall of weathered red sandstone along the road. It is, however, a mystery how a gardener of Percy's calibre could have used Leyland cypress for an internal screen. The site in question yearns for yew, which would have made a very decent hedge in ten years.

The general principle of informality called for island beds, with trees and shrubs dotted around as points of further interest. The lavish bedding schemes at which Percy shone in the public parks had no place at home. Indeed, there was an emphasis on planting for permanence, with ease of upkeep and his own advancing years in mind.

The design of the garden and the placing of the house in it make the maximum use of what is quite a dramatic site. Approaching The Magnolias from the south through the village of Bomere Heath the house is prominent, almost commanding. At the entrance to the drive it disappears from sight and remains out of view until the last few yards of the drive are reached. To the left of the drive is a border tapering towards the top, backed by a hedge which encloses the vegetable garden. This border is given to flowering trees, *Prunus ukon* among them, and substantial shrubs including at least three magnolias. To the right is lawn, dotted with Percy's much favoured island beds, with magnolias again prominent in the planting scheme. The top of the drive is dominated by roses.

The view can be glimpsed through the trees and shrubs on the way up the drive but is not fully displayed until one has passed through the house and the sun room on to the terrace. From that point the place has a pronounced upland feel. The magnificent view is almost forbidding and the hills are seen as

106

real hills, some of them indeed as mountains. Down again from the terrace into the garden, the view can either be admired in its fullness or put into a cosier perspective by moving to one of the many spots slightly enclosed by the cleverly associated plantations of shrubs which fill the island beds. In many parts of the garden a few steps in one direction or another can transform the feel of the place from the Home Counties to North Yorkshire. In this respect the garden is undisputably a triumph. That some of the borders of the sturdier shrubs at The Magnolias had not had so much as a fork in them since they were planted was a matter of some pride to Percy. The garden was generally as weedless as Eden before The Fall. This was due not to some miracle but rather to the liberal use of paraquat. Percy's prime was somewhat before the environmentalists were in full voice, although some of their favourite issues were already much discussed. Percy seemed to have little patience for them. He went on the record several times to say that the alleged deterioration in the taste of fresh vegetables should not be attributed to the use of pesticides and certain fertilizers but to the decline in popularity of the older and more culturally demanding varieties.

This ground was covered when Percy was interviewed by Roy Plomley for *Desert Island Discs* in March 1963:

Plomley: Does it worry you that nowadays, vegetables and fruit are grown in soil . . . fertilized by various chemicals instead of organic manure, and that vegetables these days, don't seem to taste of anything very much? (Laughter) They don't taste like they used to?

Percy: Yes, I heard that one so many times; they do taste

like they used to. They are different varieties,
mm. . . .

Plomley: What's happened to the good old varieties then?

Percy: They're still the good old variety, I mean, if we take . . . potatoes, we grow our – oh, people grow 'Aran Pilot' because it produces a large crop. I wouldn't grow 'Aran Pilot' – I'd grow the old 'Sharpe's Express' or 'Midlothian Early' because that is the potato that as a lad when I left school I'd almost make a meal of it if it was cooked with mint and served up with a little bit of butter.

Plomley: So shall we have to learn to look out for the right varieties – and recognize them?

Percy: Yes, you see, when you talk about a chemical fertilizer, number one is the soil, isn't it?

Plomley: Mm. . . .

Percy: . . . we've still got to keep the soil in good heart and we only keep it in good heart by putting in the humus, that . . . manure, if we can get it; garden compost is the substitute, or peat, you see? But if we start off like that, and then use the chemical fertilizer, it doesn't affect the flavour of vegetables, the flavour of fruit, or even the scent of flowers.

Plomley: What about these poisonous sprays that are used on fruit? Would you eat apples that you'd bought from a shop without peeling them?

Percy: Oh yes, I would, yes . . . there's too much said about these poisonous sprays, you know Roy, that the sprays that we use at the moment are not so poisonous as those we used to use in my early days in the garden. For instance, we used to spray

the fruit trees with lead arsenic, and what's more
poisonous than that?

Plomley: Well, there's much more spraying being done –
surely?

Percy: Ah – much more spraying being done, yes, but I
mean, DDT was introduced, that's not too
dangerous, since then BHC, and now we've got
even later introductions, the safest chemical in-
secticides are not half as dangerous as the lead
arsenic and the nicotine that we used to use.

Plomley: What about the balance of nature being upset?
We hear a lot about that.

Percy: No! I don't think so . . . Mm . . . we're only
spraying those half a dozen or a dozen roses
that we've got in the garden to keep the greenfly
or the mildew off, or the few vegetables or the
fruit – all the country side, all the way round
where the greenfly and the other insects . . .
thoroughly enjoy themselves. No, we're not
upsetting the balance of nature at all.

With the free use of chemicals went an extreme fondness for
gadgets. Percy had an easy understanding of gadgets, even
when they did not proceed beyond the trial stage at which
they were often sent to him by their manufacturers. Their
appeal to one who was brought-up with the hands-and-knees
drudgery of certain gardening processes is easy enough to
understand. Percy was also one of the very few professional
gardeners to admit to taking pleasure in cutting lawns. The
importance of good turf in a garden does not need to be
justified and the subject received its full measure of cover in
Gardeners' World when Percy would emerge to discourse,

characteristically rubbing his hands together, with even more relish than usual.

The eight years planned to make the garden at The Magnolias were not all needed to bring it to exhibition standard. The ease with which Percy absorbed the spirit of the place meant that he made relatively few errors in the choice of species or variety, and that very little ruthlessness, rethinking and re-planting was required. As he became more engrossed in the job, he later admitted, he worked obsessively hard at it. His enthusiasm infected people around him, the builder among them, who willingly joined in. This energizing example was particularly useful in enlisting the services of specialists for parts of the garden making, and for miscellaneous functions delegated in due time to his sons-in-law. Helping in the garden was one of the few reliable ways by which his daughters' boy-friends could win his confidence and, perhaps, eventually his approval.

Percy treated his sons-in-law in the same way that he treated his daughters, that is to say they were expected to do as they were told. Although all three daughters ended up involved with the running of the garden centre which their father established on the outskirts of Shrewsbury, earlier in their lives they were not pressed to take an interest or part in gardening beyond what children growing up in a garden-based family would naturally take.

The eldest daughter, Margaret, developed an early interest in flower arranging and had started a career in lecturing and demonstrating the art when she decided that she wanted to be a conventional teacher and accordingly proceeded to a training college. Her first job was at a school at Ludlow where she taught rural science, a wide-ranging subject which included a fair amount of gardening. The school gardens, which included a greenhouse and some demonstration plots, were in her charge.

Susan, the second daughter, has never, in her father's words, 'known the difference between a daisy and a dandelion'.

All three daughters married while in their twenties, although the elder two were later divorced. Susan had two sons and the youngest daughter, Ann, two daughters. Of the three sons-in-law Ann's husband Aubrey, a policeman, was probably closest to Percy in temperament and interests.

At The Magnolias, especially in the early mornings, Percy had a chance to think and to plan. Connie had very early on banned pipe smoking in their bedroom and so, as soon as he awoke, usually at around seven if he did not have to go off somewhere on the other side of the country, he went downstairs, made tea for them both, lit his pipe, and thought. After one fast, full pipe he was fit to get dressed and go outside, perhaps to start the greenhouses off for the day or attend to other diurnal rituals, always accompanied by the constant companion of his time at home, a black labrador, one or other of the succession of working gun dogs which Percy had wanted since the days when he had got to know his Dunnett grandfather's dog at Walberswick.

By the time Connie came down Percy might well have papers spread all over the kitchen table and be hard at work in his tiny handwriting. More probably he would have gone outside again, if at The Magnolias, to discuss the day's work with Sam Evans, their one full-time gardener, or if at Quarry Lodge supervising the beginning of the day's routine. The authorities at Shrewsbury in later years were far less sparing than they had been with leave of absence for Percy. They were not blind to the advantages of having a national figure in their employment and were well aware that in Percy they had one of the relatively few Salopians to have become household names. Before Percy the last such Salopian, whether by birth or adoption, to fill this role was none other than Charles Darwin; before him Lord Hill, the Duke of Wellington's right-hand man, then Clive of India, and then that paragon of sixteenth-century manhood, the soldier-poet Sir Philip Sidney. Also-rans include the retiring lady of letters, Mary Webb.

With Percy gone to his work, whether in Shrewsbury or further afield, Connie got down to keeping the domestic scene in order. Percy's dependence on her, though often expressed, was not fully realized until the time in the 1960s when she was seriously ill with brucellosis. It was only during that period, friends recall, that Percy seemed to lose his energy and self-confidence and indeed come close to grinding to a halt.

Percy had written gardening items for the local newspapers from the time he arrived at Shrewsbury. He advanced to a national audience on the invitation of Arthur Hellyer, the doyen of garden journalists, who was editor of *Amateur Gardening* at the time, and soon had Percy contracted to keep a topical guide in every issue. *Amateur Gardening* has at times during its long and distinguished history been uncertain of the level of interest and sophistication of its readers but in Hellyer's sensitive hands there was no difficulty in finding and holding the required level. Percy was less at ease with the *Sunday Express*, for which he also wrote, particularly when his editor began to call for items which 'Lord Copper', the arbitrary newspaper proprietor in Evelyn Waugh's novel *Scoop*, might have described as 'peppy', despite the fact that the readers appeared to be perfectly happy with the natural and

Shrewsbury Show, the second most important flower show in Britain, in the late 1940s, showing the new limes, planted by Percy, along the river bank. The large hollow called the Dingle is concealed by the trees behind the bandstand.

Percy with judges at the 1949 Shrewsbury Show. *From left:* Gen. Sir Oliver Leese (a pillar of the show and cacti enthusiast), Roland Smith, Charles Cook (*Shropshire Horticultural Society).*

Percy with Roland Smith, head gardener to the Earl of Bradford, at Weston-under-Lizard in the late 1940s after a wireless broadcast. In the early days Percy's programmes would often revolve around a visit to a distinguished garden and a chat to its keeper.

Percy outside Quarry Lodge, Percy and Connie's home in Shrewsbury from 1946 to the early 1960s *(Reveille Newspapers Ltd Jack Curtis)*.

Percy with Godfrey Baseley *(right)*, the man who recognized Percy's broadcasting talents, and Barrie Edgar, the producer with whom he worked both at the beginning and end of his career, discussing an early television broadcast.

Although Percy was initially very nervous at the idea of being on air he soon came to enjoy broadcasting. He later said he was more nervous reading the lesson in church. *Above: Gardeners' World* production team at Percy's last home, The Magnolias, near Shrewsbury. Producer Bill Duncalf (in striped shirt) is in the centre. Many broadcasts came from Percy's very own garden (*Amateur Gardening*).

Percy being fitted with a concealed microphone for a broadcast. Percy never worked from a script, even for live broadcasts (*Amateur Gardening*).

Percy attending to a fuschia — a plant which he did much to popularize.

A pause between takes for *Gardeners' World*. Percy with Arthur Billitt, at Arthur's home, Clack's Farm, Worcestershire. Percy and Arthur became a lovable double act and Clack's Farm a popular location for the series.

Making the garden of The Magnolias. After years of tending other people's, Percy relished having his own.

The first open day at The Magnolias, 1966. Over 5,000 people turned up — a fraction of the number who flocked in later years creating traffic chaos in the neighbourhood.

Percy enjoyed the company of his colleagues at ICI almost as much as at the BBC. It was a matter of some sadness to him when the two activities became incompatible. Here he is with *from left:* Dr Jo Stubbs, Peter König, Toby Hicks *(ICI Garden Products).*

With the Queen Mother at the opening of the Syon Park Garden Centre, 1968.

The growth of garden centres from the 1960s onwards was partly due to a new enthusiasm for gardening generated by Percy and others. Here is is at his own centre in Shrewsbury.

Britain's 'head gardener' with Connie, at The Magnolias, 1975.

logical programme that Percy was offering them. He consequently left the paper, although he resumed with the same
group and contributions for the northern edition of the *Daily
Express*.

One problem which his early newspaper editors had was
how to translate his highly individual style and tone of voice
on to the page. It was not really solved until he progressed to
writing books, first for Collingridge and then for Hamlyn, by
whom they were taken over in 1967. The simple answer,
which his Collingridge editor, Robert Pearson (now gardening correspondent of *The Sunday Telegraph*), devised, was to
face up to a little extra work at the publishing end of the
process by allowing Percy to dictate his material. Collingridge
acquired a tape-recorder especially for the purpose. Percy
invariably put far more on to the tapes than was strictly
necessary and this helped to make the eventual result, skil-
fully edited into print, all the more rewarding. The tape-
recorder soon became the preferred means of drafting his
newspaper articles as well. For this purpose, in contrast to the
preparation of books, Percy's method of work was highly
disciplined. The recorded piece would run to the required
wordage, neither more nor less, with the whole punctuated
and paragraphed as naturally and necessarily as if he were
pausing for breath. By this method, Percy was as immediately
effective and present when read as when heard.

With the books, in particular, the publishers, the author
and, in a different way, the readers, struck gold. It is un-
accountably difficult to say exactly how many books Percy
wrote because so many of them appeared in different re-
visions, arrangements and formats. At the time of his death
there could definitely be said to be eleven books to his name.
They sold prodigiously. One of the most popular, *Every Day*

Gardening in Colour, originally published in 1969, had by the time of its revised edition in 1988 sold one and a half million copies.

The bibliography of British gardening is huge and distinguished. Why Percy came to occupy quite so large a place in it can once again be attributed to a certain degree of luck. The readership was there, willing and eager to be told how to garden with the minimum of pain for the maximum effect; publishing technology happened to be at the stage where lavish colour illustration, with working instructions and drawings exactly integrated with the text, was practicable; above all Percy was on television at least once a week, telling everybody what to do and how to do it again, and enthusing them to go forth and continue their colloquy, book in hand, in the intimacy of the potting-shed.

For most of his life Percy was far too involved in getting through the volume of work that fell to him to have much opportunity to reflect on his lot. Far from being a sanctuary, even The Magnolias was a more or less continuous hubbub of work and commitments arising from the work. By 1966, far sooner than expected, the garden was ready to be shown to the public, the first of a series of open days for charitable ends. On that first Sunday five thousand people turned up; but as the garden, as well as its owner, began to appear on *Gardeners' World* the numbers drawn to open days increased, creating problems with traffic and, in particular, parking in the scattered location of Bomere Heath. Fortunately the goodwill of some of the farmers helped solve the parking problem through the loan of fields as temporary car parks. As the numbers of visitors grew they were tightly packed. On the very busiest afternoon that Percy could remember there were about forty charabancs as well as the cars, and having sold their stock of seven thousand five hundred tickets the total number of visitors could only be estimated and was thought to be nearly ten thousand. Percy made a habit of climbing into the entrance of each coach as it arrived to introduce himself (perhaps superfluously) and welcome the passengers to his garden. This gesture paid dividends, for while garden enthusiasts are generally good sorts there were obvious risks of damage from having so many people passing over a relatively small space in a few hours. Playing the host on these occasions did not come as easily to him as it appeared. He was essentially quite a shy man in the sense that he did not like to push himself forward. Thus, it was one thing to be invited and paid to stand in front of a television camera and talk, quite another to impose himself on people who had been kind enough – as he saw it – to take an interest in his own garden. Being on display at home came slightly more easily to Connie, for although she definitely did not enjoy the limelight, her parents' house at Windsor had been something of a goldfish bowl and she could thus accept the presence of curious strangers as part of the order of things.

At the end of each open day there was seldom a spent fag-end to be seen, let alone any evidence of thieving or other villainy. Only the grass looked a bit sad, although most of the parts trodden by the public were of field grass, which Percy had spent many happy hours taming. There were other areas of fine grass which Percy had sown around the house itself.

With the open-day visitors gone and the down-trodden grass exhaling in the dew, there might be a pause of no more than a few days before a television crew of up to forty personnel, with many tons of expensive equipment, arrived to record for *Gardeners' World*. These sessions were most commonly on Tuesdays, with two programmes being recorded in the day. On such a schedule there was no room for amateurism or time for retakes. Given eighty seconds in which to cover the propagation of fuchsias, for example, even with everything planned and pots, rooting powder and composts to hand, both the presenter and the producer had to perform with tremendous poise and efficiency, particularly if they were to avoid the slightest suggestion of haste, which is anathema to any garden process. There were mishaps, though few that were allowed to go beyond embarrassment to disaster. On one occasion Percy was knee-deep in *Hypericum calycinum*, poised to demonstrate how to keep this excellent but invasive ground cover under control. The essential shears were lying on the edge of the adjacent grass, in full view of the camera, though from Percy's standpoint in dead ground. Unable to ask for or receive instructions he improvised his way off the scene.

The garden of The Magnolias had been made partly with television in mind. *Gardeners' World*, indeed, followed its making and was used by Percy as a model through which to convey a step-by-step account of garden making: how to tame the soil and create a microclimate by the judicious planting of hedges and large shrubs; how to discover and exploit the genius of a site, however small, by close observation and experiment; how to plant for both immediate and long term effect; and always how to achieve perfection with the minimum of hands-and-knees drudgery. It had its limitations, however, particularly when cameras advanced and became more mobile, because parts of the garden were difficult to get at. At times, a special platform had to be built in the drive for some of the equipment. The vegetable garden, to Percy a thing of beauty equal in its way to the pleasure garden, was particularly problematical for access. In a season of *Gardeners'*

World perhaps no more than six programmes would actually be filmed at The Magnolias, but given the greed of television even that was quite enough from an editorial point of view.

The programme was broadcast from many other places – Forde Abbey in Dorset, the Savill Garden in Windsor Great Park, Hever Castle in Kent, Nymans in Sussex, Grayswood Hill in Surrey, Crathes Castle on Deeside being some of the favourites – but thanks, in part, to the foresight of the producer, Bill Duncalf, it came to have a second home at Clack's Farm, near Droitwich in Worcestershire, on probably the finest, and certainly the most blandly seductive, horticultural land in England. If The Magnolias was Eden after The Fall on a good day, Clack's Farm was Paradise regained.

Arthur Billitt had bought Clack's Farm in the 1950s when he was still working for Boots as director of their Lenton Research Centre near Nottingham. He had been peripherally involved with *Gardening Club*, growing material for use on the programme while still at Lenton. His work on the garden at Clack's Farm, which until his retirement from Boots in 1967 had been entirely on the flower garden, had been a herculean part-time job on the part of his wife and himself, with occasional unskilled help from outside. In the autumn after Arthur's retirement from Boots Bill Duncalf called on him at Clack's Farm and, sniffing out the potential, sowed the idea of a made-for-television vegetable garden on part of the abundant land that was so far scarcely cultivated. The scheme was pressed ahead, perhaps slightly more quickly than was quite welcome to Arthur, and the new garden was first seen on television during the following season. In due time the familiar geometrical grid of beds separated by broad, paved paths took shape. Parts of the completion and planting of the vegetable and fruit gardens joined the *Gardeners' World* schedule.

Here Arthur and Percy appeared in what must be the most endearing double act yet seen on British television. Percy's configuration was not ideal for television. In height, at slightly under six feet, he was on the tall side of average, but there was disproportionately little of that height in his legs, which were short, and rather a lot in his head, which was large – especially the deep forehead, which housed the capacious and deceptively agile mind. As to the hands, which are always a problem when on display, Percy was happiest with them fully occupied demonstrating some garden task. Arthur, by contrast, was the philosopher of the act – smaller, slighter and an altogether less powerful presence than Percy, seven or eight years his senior in age but like him looking no more than fifty – standing characteristically with one arm behind his back, the other free to gesture in his discourse, apparently unaware that he and Percy were there to do anything but talk between themselves.

'Wonderful thing, mother nature . . . isn't she Percy?'

'Yes, yes, Arthur. Now. About these potatoes.'

Nothing could deflect Percy from the subject in hand. During one live broadcast in the early spring of 1960 he had been warned to expect an interruption for a news flash. It duly came, announcing the engagement of Princess Margaret. The camera presently returned to Percy, smiling smugly in the manner of one who had known all about it: 'Now. Back to the gooseberries.' The producers of *Gardeners' World*, Barrie Edgar in particular, well appreciated the delicious material in front of them and pushed their skills to the limit to make the most of it.

Percy's easy authority and single-mindedness in the programme attracted a certain amount of criticism, especially his tendency to take the lead over specialist guests. Some arbiters of taste within the BBC, moved primarily by the mindless pursuit of pointless innovation, began to suggest that Percy might be 'rested'. Percy, too, was tired – in the sense that he had given nearly everything he had to give to his role – but in the event he was led away from *Gardeners' World*, though not from the BBC for ever, by other developments in his career.

There was a time when Percy was such a substantial presence on the television screen that he could have begun to neglect his garden base and make his way as a miscellaneous personality of the medium. Had he reached his prime twenty years later that, alas, is very possibly the direction in which he would have gone saved only, perhaps, by Connie's voice of calm restraint in all things and his own awareness that out of his natural element he might wither into nothing. What exactly makes an acceptable television character, let alone a magnetic one, has so far defied exact analysis. Percy was certainly a man whom the people manifestly welcomed into their gardens, in a manner of speaking, and it seems equally likely that he would have been as welcome and as readily at home in their sitting-rooms. The men accepted him as one who would make excellent company for an evening in the pub (a place where not a few of Percy's evenings were spent). He was attractive to women from quite an early age and this attraction did not lose its power when he was distanced by the television screen.

At Clack's Farm there is a five-barred gate upon which Percy and Arthur sometimes rested or posed during a recording of *Gardeners' World*. Lady visitors to Clack's Farm on open days would make for this gate and if necessary form a queue to file past, touching the top rail rather as if it were an icon in an

Orthodox church. Equally exotically, Percy's way with plants attracted the admiration of the Swedish actress Mai Zetterling whose husband, possibly bored by having Percy quoted all the time, induced him to write to his wife about her lilies. He duly did so and the letter was much appreciated; so much so that when in 1976 Percy was given that bizarre accolade of popular approval, an edition of *This Is Your Life*, Mai Zetterling was specially flown in to meet her hero for the first time. It was manifest from the programme that the actuality of Percy did not disappoint her. Such gestures of appreciation were a small part of Percy's reward which lay, as it had always done, in making a living out of what was coincidentally his hobby.

His popularity on television inevitably led him to have to take, as it were, work home with him. Every programme brought in a huge number of letters, most of which were directed to the BBC in Birmingham who mostly dealt with them, leaving Percy and his one secretary to handle those sent direct to Shrewsbury. 'Britain's head gardener' also received a large number of enquiries from people who wrote to him simply because of his perceived authority and not as a result of a comment on a programme. A quite staggering proportion of these letters – often with photographs or specimens enclosed – were from people who had grown what seemed to be a unique plant from a standard packet of seed supposedly of a known variety. The explanation was usually a stray or rogue seed in a packet, and these enquirers Percy could only direct for attention to one of the seedsmen such as Sutton's.

Other enquiries received a full and generous answer, dictated heaven knows when. The following letter, in reply to a highly intelligent letter from Porthcawl on the South Wales coast following a visit to the Dingle, is a fair example:

I thank you for your letter and was delighted to hear that you enjoyed the Pink and Purple flower bed in the Dingle last summer.

The Fibrous rooted begonia was Begonia Semperfloren Thousand Wonders. These are grown from seeds in late February or early March in a temperature of 60 to 65 degrees. The Heliotrope, W. H. Lowther, is grown from cuttings but it is possible to grow Heliotrope from seed sown at the same time as the Begonias. I would suggest that you write to Thompson & Morgan Ltd, Nurserymen and Seedsmen, London Road, Ipswich, or to Sutton & Sons Ltd, The Royal Seed Establishment, Reading.

So long as the bed is protected from the strong winds from the sea then I see no reason why these plants should not do well.

Subsequently, it transpired that this correspondent had difficulty in obtaining the stocks she wanted and in the end Percy sent them to her himself.

Other somewhat gnomic questions received very down to earth replies:

Question: If somebody gave you the money to buy a compost bin, which sort would you buy?
Answer: Four posts and some wire netting.

It was important to Percy that the people with whom he worked should be congenial. This was part of the pleasure in his long association with the BBC. The succession of producers with whom he worked were all, partly by reason of their generation and partly by reason of the nature of the BBC when they joined it, people of the sort who might be found in the officers' mess of a good, though not necessarily fashionable, regiment. Though a robust individualist, Percy rejoiced in the *esprit de corps* that often goes with a well-run institution. For this reason he was to find ICI, or more exactly its subsidiary Plant Protection Ltd, thoroughly agreeable. He described his contract with them, entered into at the beginning of 1961, as 'the best I ever signed'.

Percy was well aware of the BBC's reservations about anything untouched by the pellucid grace of impartiality. Back in the 1951 General Election campaign, early in his broadcasting career, he had been warned not to refer by name to a favoured Michaelmas daisy because it was called 'Winston Churchill'. He also knew that Arthur Billitt's path to early stardom – had he sought it – had been blocked by his position with Boots, although oddly enough C. H. Middleton himself had had a promotion-by-association deal with Boots of the sort that Percy had now entered into with Plant Protection. Odder still, Plant Protection had in the thirties tried to net Middleton for themselves but, much to their chagrin, had failed to produce a formula slippery enough to get round the BBC. Before Percy had actually signed with Plant Protection the late Sir Anthony Hurd, Member of Parliament for Newbury and a director of Fisons Fertilisers, one of Plant Protection's rivals, had questioned the propriety of the proposed arrangement. As he had no contract with the BBC, what Percy did elsewhere was largely a matter of honour and convenience. However, he undertook not to advertise for ICI or otherwise embarrass the BBC, and made it plain to both sides that he would feel free to criticize Plant Protection products if he thought fit, and on that basis the deal went ahead.

ICI had a programme of speeches and events at which Percy was to appear and over a period of twenty years cover the whole country. At these events Percy spoke, signed copies of his books, and did everything that he might do at a local horticultural show, while the Plant Protection products stood in displays round about. The product which attracted most interest in the garden world at the time was 'Weedol', otherwise known as the 'chemical hoe', which had the miraculous power to kill weeds among plants without being activated by the soil. That was the nature and extent of his work for ICI.

The temptation to proceed a stage further, into actual advertising and, furthermore, advertising on television, increased as the years passed and Percy finally succumbed during 1975. The television commercials – for 'Rose Plus', 'Lawn Plus', 'Garden Plus', 'Weedol' and 'Pathclear' – involved a style of work that was quite unfamiliar to him and of a sort which he had often deplored. Exactly scripted and shot and reshot until they reached the level of perfection peculiar to advertising, the thirty-eight-second commercials required up to twenty-five takes each, spread over three days. The cost of this to Percy was sudden and permanent banishment from *Gardeners' World*. The decision had been entirely his own and was taken in full knowledge of the consequences.

Typically, it was only on the morning after that the gap left by his departure settled into sharp outline. The highly experienced substitutes on *Gardeners' World*, many of them long familiar as excellent lieutenants, looked reduced and fragile for many months. Percy has never really been replaced as the voice and face and hands of British gardening. It was, after all, as the current chairman of *Gardeners' Question Time*, Clay Jones, has put it, 'Percy who taught us all how to do it'.

Would Percy now stand a chance of reaching the position he did as the instructor and arbiter of taste in one of the most popular of this country's leisure pursuits? Put another way, if the BBC was in search of a new voice of gardening, would anybody put their head round the office door of a young parks superintendent in a provincial town? The answer is that it is regrettably unlikely. There was a pioneering innocence amongst television producers in the days when Percy shot through its ranks, which was shared to some degree in the perception of the people who watched it. When this went it was replaced by a cynical reluctance to accept anybody who appears to have everything to offer in a specialized field. It is perhaps the measure of his uniqueness, even in his time, that Percy won that acceptance.

8

The Gardening Year

In the course of a review of *Gardeners' World* in 1972 the *Daily Telegraph*'s then television critic, Sean Day-Lewis, described Percy as 'a natural teacher'.

The wide-ranging fund of knowledge and expertise on which Percy drew was rooted in a way of life that was largely remote from anything known to his hearers. By the time his audience reached its largest in the early 1970s, the number of private estates with a full hierarchy of gardeners on the staff was reduced to a few dozen and there was no scent in the air of the revival these estates are currently enjoying, whether as working entities or as live museums, such as the brilliant reconstruction by the BBC and Harry Dodson for the series *The Victorian Kitchen Garden* towards the end of 1987.

On the ordinary domestic scene, gardens became ever smaller. Owners of large and unmanageable gardens found property developers eager to relieve them of the burden. Thus the vegetable garden, the tennis court and the rose garden of a house in a once spacious suburb became the site of three or more houses, each with its few square yards of ground for the new owners to make their own. These plots were generally very much smaller than the areas of front and back garden which had been a feature of most developments of semi-detached houses between the two wars. A lot of Percy's time as a broadcaster or journalist had been given to encouraging people to make the most of these plots, which were often no longer than the length of a clothes-line nor more than a few paces wide. The presence of an area of vegetables in what was predominantly a flower garden did not detract from the beauty of the whole. 'A well-kept vegetable garden,' Percy often said, 'is just as beautiful as a flower garden.' The increasing interest in vegetable growing which came – and stayed – from the self-sufficiency craze of the early 1970s was thus a matter of pleasure and satisfaction to him. Now, in many small gardens, flowers and vegetables would be cultivated and displayed as rightful peers.

Percy seldom bothered actually to say that there was always something to do in a garden. Yet his own annual schedule in the garden was quite forbiddingly full. He set it out by example, by word or in writing many times, of which the following summary, from *In Your Garden With Percy Thrower*, is a fair example:

January

First week: Top-dress lawns. Read the new catalogues. Renew grease bands. Prune outdoor vines. Dig vegetable garden. Make hot beds. Prepare for chrysanthemum cuttings. Stake pot-grown bulbs.

Second week: Repair lawns. Prepare ground for outdoor chrysanthemums. Force chicory and rhubarb. Sprout seed potatoes. Sow vegetables in heated frame. Clean greenhouse. Take chrysanthemum cuttings. Remove faded flowers from azaleas.

Third week: Order herbaceous perennials. Tie in raspberry canes. Remove canker wounds. Feed blackcurrants. Prune gooseberries. Sow vegetables under cloches. Start to force pot-grown strawberries. Sow onions under glass. Prune fuchsias. Top-dress vine borders.

Fourth week: Replant herbaceous borders. Protect sweet

peas. Prune ornamental trees. Protect primulas from birds. Prune newly-planted fruit bushes. Protect peas and beans from mice. Make first greenhouse sowings. Repot fuchsias. Take cuttings of perpetual-flowering carnations.

February

First week: Prune winter-flowering shrubs. Make and plant rock gardens. Prune cobnuts. Feed fruit trees. Prepare asparagus beds. Sow vegetables under cloches. Sow peas and runner beans in pots. Start dahlia tubers. Prune and repot pelargoniums.

Second week: Feed herbaceous plants. Plant lilies. Protect gooseberry bushes. Top-dress asparagus beds. Plant shallots. Feed spring cabbages. Divide herbs. Sow sweet peas and asparagus fern. Pot up indoor crysanthemums.

Third week: Plant lilies-of-the-valley. Replace old shrubs. Prune buddleias. Protect apricot and peach flowers. Prune autumn-fruiting raspberries. Transplant autumn-sown onions. Sow peas. Lime vegetable garden. Take fuchsia and verbena cuttings. Sow lupins and delphiniums.

Fourth week: Prune willows and dogwoods. Spray roses for black spot. Prune fig trees. Spray peach trees against leaf curl. Sow Brussels sprouts, cabbages, leeks, lettuces and radishes. Sow gloxinias and tuberous begonias. Reduce vine shoots.

March

First week: Divide snowdrops. Plant herbaceous perennials and hardy cyclamen. Polinate peach and apricot trees. Sow onions, parsnips and broad beans. Stop fuchsias. Take dahlia cuttings. Start begonia and gloxinia tubers. Take outdoor chrysanthemum cuttings.

Second week: Sow hardy annuals. Prune large-flowered clematis. Feed lawns. Feed raspberries, loganberries, blackberries and strawberries. Prepare celery trenches. Sow summer and autumn cabbages. Feed pot-grown hydrangeas. Stop mid-season chrysanthemums. Sow tomatoes.

Third week: Prune, spray and feed roses. Plant gladiolus corms. Remove protection from alpines. Mulch wall-trained fruit. Spray blackcurrants. Sow leeks and carrots. Feed winter lettuces. Feed annuals in pots. Divide ferns. Pot up outdoor chrysanthemum cuttings.

Fourth week: Sow pansies and violas. Prune early-flowering shrubs. Sow sweet peas. Graft fruit trees. Spray pears against scrab. Plant potatoes and mint. Sow peas and parsnips. Plant onion sets. Sow greenhouse primulas. Sow half-hardy annuals.

April

First week: Take cuttings of herbaceous perennials. Mow lawns. Spray peaches against aphids. Mulch raspberries, blackberries and loganberries. Plant asparagus. Plant maincrop potatoes. Sow parsley. Complete sowing of half-hardy annuals. Sow tomatoes, celery and celeriac.

Second week: Sow new lawns. Plant sweet peas and biennials. Prune forsythias. Plant clematis. Disbud peaches and apricots. Spray gooseberries and pears. Sow asparagus and carrots. Earth up peas and broad beans. Sow melons and cucumbers. Tie in vine rods.

Third week: Prepare ground for outdoor chrysanthemums. Remove dead heads from daffodils, pansies and violas. Layer rhododendrons and azaleas. Spray raspberries and apples. Plant maincrop potatoes. Make up hanging baskets. Stake pot-grown lilies. Side-shoot tomatoes.

Fourth week: Plant dahlia tubers. Spot treat lawns. Plant water lilies. Protect strawberries. Spray plums. Disbud peaches. Earth up early potatoes. Sow sweet corn and marrows. Prick out half-hardy annuals and tomatoes. Stop vines.

May

First week: Stake herbaceous perennials. Train sweet peas. Plant outdoor chrysanthemums. Tie in peach shoots. Examine fruit tree grafts. Plant out Brussels sprouts. Sow sweet corn, endive and chicory. Harden off bedding plants. Plant tomatoes in greenhouse border.

Second week: Sow half-hardy annuals. Stop outdoor chrysanthemums. Train rambler roses. Water newly-planted trees and shrubs. Spray blackcurrants. Straw strawberries. Thin apricots. Plant melons. Hoe onions. Sow French and runner beans. Shade greenhouse.

Third week: Remove dead heads from bulbs. Spray roses. Apply weedkiller to lawns. Prick out polyanthus. Bark ring apple trees. Water well-trained fruit. Prepare frames for cucumbers. Rest cyclamen corms. Pot on begonias and gloxinias.

Fourth week: Prepare summer bedding. Lift and divide primulas. Prepare ground for dahlia cuttings. Thin raspberry canes. Spray apple trees. Net strawberries. Plant runner beans and cucumbers. Prepare ground for marrows. Stake and feed verbenas. Take pelargonium cuttings.

June

First week: Water bedding plants. Stake herbaceous plants and lilies. Spray roses. Sow biennials. Spray raspberries. Pick gooseberries. Spray cherries. Plant marrows, celery and celeriac. Sow turnips. Plant outdoor tomatoes. Rest Arum lilies. Start poinsettias.

Second week: Cut grass edges. Trim alpines. Lift tulips. Tie in blackberries and loganberries. Train cordon gooseberries. Stop and top-dress cucumbers. Stop broad beans. Lift early potatoes. Thin grapes. Stop mid-season chrysanthemums. Stake tuberous begonias.

Third week: Dead-head lupins and delphiniums. Disbud roses. Prick out aubrietas and alyssums. Sow winter-flowering pansies. Stop outdoor vines. Thin apricots. Protect cherries from birds. Plant leeks and cabbages. Pick tomatoes regularly. Spray carnations.

Fourth week: Divide irises. Take cuttings of alpines. Feed lawns. Prune early-flowering shrubs. Thin overcrowded fruit trees. Pick raspberries. Reduce strawberry runners. Protect cauliflower curds. Spray French and runner beans. Plunge azaleas outside. Fumigate against whitefly.

July

First week: Feed roses and chrysanthemums. Clip privet hedges. Divide hardy primulas. Peg down strawberry runners. Water celery. Spray potatoes. Prune hydrangeas. Tie in chrysanthemums. Disbud tuberous begonias. Take leaf cuttings of begonias.

Second week: Layer border carnations. Take begonia cuttings. Feed and mulch dahlias. Thin overcrowded fruit trees. Thin outdoor grapes and spray against mildew. Sow endive, spinach beet and seakale beet.

Third week: Prick out biennials. Thin dahlias. Bud roses. Spray gooseberries. Prune and feed blackcurrants. Prune trained apple trees. Protect morello cherries from birds. Destroy eggs of cabbage white butterflies. Spray celery against leaf spot and celery fly. Stop outdoor tomatoes.

Fourth week: Take half-ripe cuttings of shrubs. Bud fruit trees. Prepare ground for strawberries. Remove plum branches infected with silver leaf. Feed and water cucumbers and melons. Lift shallots and garlic. Gather herbs for drying. Start cyclamen into growth.

August

First week: Disbud dahlias and outdoor chrysanthemums. Trim laurel hedges. Plant Madonna lilies. Train wisterias. Water celery and runner beans. Bend onion tops over. Spray peas. Spray cyclamen in frames. Remove lower leaves from tomatoes.

Second week: Collect and sow seeds of hardy primulas and meconopsis. Retrain cordon sweet peas. Prune raspberries. Sow spring cabbages and onions. Earth up celery. Pot up pelargonium cuttings. Feed ferns.

Third week: Take cuttings of zonal pelargoniums. Protect dahlias from earwigs. Remove rose suckers. Cut and dry 'everlasting' flowers. Select strawberry plants for forcing next year. Pick early apples. Order Christmas bulbs. Sow cyclamen.

Fourth week: Plant border carnations. Prune rambler roses. Trim lavender bushes. Protect chrysanthemum blooms. Prepare compost heap. Remove strawberry runners. Sow winter lettuce. Prepare ground for winter cabbage. Disbud chrysanthemums.

September

First week: Take lavender and rose cuttings. Plant daffodils and cut flowers. Transplant violets. Prepare to store apples and pears. Gather French and runner beans and sweet corn. Remove early cyclamen flowers. Sow greenhouse annuals.

Second week: Plant bulbs for naturalizing. Prune rampant climbers. Train climbing roses. Treat hydrangeas with colourant. Pick apples and pears. Ripen onions. Feed leeks. Pot cyclamen. Re-house Arum lilies.

Third week: Protect alpines with panes of glass. Expose grapes to sun. Prune loganberries. Lift and store carrots and beetroot. Clear away greenhouse tomatoes. House cyclamen. Dry off begonias and gloxinias. Pot up bulbs.

Fourth week: Propagate tender bedding plants. Lift gladioli. Sow sweet peas. Hoe strawberry beds. Earth up celery and leeks. Store onions. Lift maincrop potatoes. Pick outdoor tomatoes. House freesias, carnations and chrysanthemums. Prick out greenhouse annuals.

October

First week: Rake lawns. Lift tender plants. Prune rambler roses. Thin raspberry canes. Take gooseberry cuttings. Plant lettuces in frames. Pick runner and French beans. Plant spring cabbages. House chrysanthemums. Pot pre-cooled bulbs for Christmas.

Second week: Prepare ground for spring bedding. Pot up shrub cuttings. Complete picking of apples and pears and inspect those in store. Prepare ground for fruit trees. Prune blackberries. Store begonia and gloxinia tubers. House hydrangeas and fuchsias.

Third week: Plant spring bedding, aubrietas, alyssum and winter-flowering pansies. Take cuttings of shrubs and roses. Clean strawberry beds. Tie in raspberries. Prune and train morello cherries. Turn compost heaps. Lift seakale. Put up lilies.

Fourth week: Tidy the herbaceous border. Lift and store dahlia tubers. Complete bulb planting. Inspect fruit in store. Lift roots of parsley for winter use. Cut down asparagus. Pot roses for the greenhouse. Dry off Canna lilies.

November

First week: Tidy up the garden. Lay turf. Plant lilies. Protect tender shrubs. Clean and grease lawn mowers. Prune red and white currants. Ridge heavy soils. Lift Jerusalem artichokes, parsnips and horseradish. Pot up lilies-of-the-valley.

Second week: Lift and protect outdoor chrysanthemums. Plant lily-of-the-valley crowns. Plant hedges. Prune apples and pears. Plant fruit trees. Sow broad beans and hardy peas. Cut down chrysanthemums.

Third week: Plant ornamental trees and waterside plants. Prune neglected fruit trees. Rake up fallen leaves. Plant red and white currants. Hoe between lettuce and onions. Cut Savoy cabbages. Bring pots of bulbs out of plunge beds.

Fourth week: Repair and re-lay garden paths. Plant rhododendrons and azaleas. Protect Christmas roses. Plant raspberries, blackberries and loganberries. Protect trees from mice. Inspect fruit and potatoes in store. Force rhubarb and chicory.

December

First week: Half-prune roses. Ventilate plants in frames. Protect delphiniums from slugs. Repair fences. Control big bud on blackcurrants. Prune outdoor vines. Lift celery. Earth up spring cabbages. Box up chrysanthemum stools. Bring pots of bulbs into greenhouse.

Second week: Treat wooden fences with preservative. Cut winter-flowering shrubs for the house. Continue to plant trees and shrubs. Screen newly-planted evergreens. Order winter washes. Inspect grease bands. Force seakale. Protect broccoli. Sow onions. Sponge foliage plants.

Third week: Shake snow off trees and shrubs. Paint garden frames. Firm cuttings. Apply winter wash to fruit trees, and feed. Lift leeks and heel in. Force rhubarb. Prepare ground for runner beans. Prune vines and peaches under glass. Take carnation cuttings.

Fourth week: Order flower seeds. Dig over annual borders.

Check protective material used on tender plants. Protect fruit against bird damage. Manure wall-trained fruit trees. Force mint. Prepare onion bed. Cut back pelargoniums. Clean greenhouse thoroughly.

This was a programme for an extreme enthusiast – for a fanatic, in fact – and one with a large, fully-equipped garden. There is within it, however, a schedule which anybody with any sort of garden could usefully follow, and there was the same simplicity and directness in the explanatory and guiding notes which Percy provided in many forms and in many places from a simple routine task, such as keeping the green-house clean and disease-free to arts as recondite and, frankly, tricky as budding roses. Here he is on the matter of digging, which he manages to make sound not only simpler than it ever proves to be in practice but also a pleasure:

Double digging is the most satisfactory preparation. This means thoroughly breaking up the soil to a depth of about two feet. The work is commenced by making a two foot-wide trench across the plot to a depth of one foot and wheeling the soil removed from this to the other end of the patch. Then the gardener gets into the trench and, with a strong digging fork, breaks up the bottom soil as deeply as possible. The work proceeds by opening an adjacent trench two feet in width and turning the soil on to the broken soil lying in the previous trench. Now the bottom of this new trench is forked.

So the work goes on, two foot strip by two foot strip, until the far end of the bed is reached, when the heap of soil removed from the first trench will be used to fill up the last trench.

On a more obviously appealing subject, such as the making of rock gardens, he was not only seductive but in five short paragraphs comprehensive, saying all that anybody with any feeling for gardening would need to know and leaving ample scope for individual imagination:

A rock garden is not merely a haphazard collection of pieces of rock or lumps of concrete, sticking up at all angles, with pockets of soil in between in which dwarf plants languish. A properly constructed rock garden should, as far as poss-ible, look like a natural outcrop of rocks and give the impression that the rocks seen above the surface are part of a more extensive body of rock that lies beneath – like an iceberg, which has most of its bulk below water level. To give the right impression it is not necessary to have enor-mous lumps of stone – quite small pieces are sufficient, although one or two large pieces can be helpful to provide the keystones around which the rock garden is built.

To get this natural effect it is best to use stone with well-defined lines or strata. Water-worn Cumberland limestone and certain hard sandstones are the best. Granite and marble are the most unsuitable types. The rocks are laid so that the strata lines run approximately in the same direction. Although this is easier when you build the rock garden on a bank, many successful gardens have been built on the flat. Try to ensure that the garden is built in a series of rough steps and this will leave pockets of soil behind each layer to accommodate plants. These can be filled with lime-free soil for lime-hating plants, peat for peat-lovers etc., or you can put in deep beds of gritty soil for those that like sharp drainage. But ordinary garden soil will do for most alpine plants. Crevices left between the rocks can be used to plant alpines which will create a natural effect. As the plants are supplied in pots it is possible to plant at almost any time of the year, even when the plants are in flower. If they are, though, shade them from strong sunshine for a day or two after planting.

Be careful when moving heavy rocks into position or you may injure yourself. When positioning really large ones it is necessary to use a block and tackle and boards. It is important when laying the rocks to make sure that they are seated firmly, packing soil behind and around each one. This will not only prevent the stones wobbling but it will ensure that there are no air pockets into which the roots may penetrate and die.

After the rock garden has been completed it is a good plan to top-dress the soil. Where lime-hating plants are being grown peat makes a good top-dressing. In fact peat can be used for all plants as it helps to retain moisture and is gradually absorbed into the soil to improve its consistency. If the natural soil is on the heavy side coarse sand can be worked in with a hand fork. Where the natural soil is poor it is best to remove it and replace it with a prepared compost of soil, moist peat and coarse sand.

Planting between the rocks must be done carefully with a small trowel or handfork. Make sure that the soil is firmed evenly. Numerous small shrubs and conifers are suitable for planting on rock gardens and these should be planted first. Do not plant too closely as many alpine plants spread rapidly.

Of fuchsia stopping, recommended as a job for the first week of March, he wrote:

Fuchsias which were pruned earlier should now be making several growths. To ensure that you obtain bushy plants, or, if you have standard specimens, that they have fine heads, pinch out the top of each shoot when it has produced four to six pairs of leaves. If standard fuchsias are required for planting out later on, this tipping also enables them to stand up to wind much better than if the shoots were allowed to grow long without being stopped.

There were simple remedial measures for problems which might perplex some gardeners for years:

Apple trees sometimes grow very strongly and produce few flowers. This means that crops will be poor and one way to curb the growth is to bark ring the trees. If the whole tree is growing too vigorously the ring of bark can be taken out from around the main stem, but if one branch has a tendency to grow strongly it is only necessary to ring the branch concerned. The ring must be no more than half an inch wide, and should go down as far as the wood. Afterwards, seal the cut with adhesive tape.

Then there was the ubiquitous problem of rose suckers:

I keep a close lookout throughout the year for suckers growing from the roots below the union of the rose and the rootstock. Despite the fact that there are several distinctive features by which suckers may be recognised, I often see them allowed to reach considerable size before being removed. Briar suckers have small, pale green leaves, and those from the rugosa stock can be identified by their rough, crinkled leaves and dense stem covering prickle-like spines. Suckers of *Rosa laxa* and *Rosa polyantha*, the other popular rose stocks, are both fairly distinct from the growth of garden roses, but whenever I am in doubt I trace the stem back to its point of origin. If this is below the point of budding, recognisable on bushes, climbers and ramblers as a slight swelling or irregularity in the main stem just above the roots and usually below soil level, I then know that the shoot is a sucker. Standard roses are worked high up on the main stem of the stock and so all shoots below the head of branches are suckers and must be removed as soon as these are noticed.

9

Britain's Head Gardener

'He who would be happy for life,' the Chinese proverb has it, 'should be a gardener.' Whenever he thought of his retirement Percy had always imagined that the greater part of it would be spent in the cultivation and enjoyment of his acre and a half at The Magnolias. For one whose work was his hobby conventional retirement was never in view. At the time he retired from his post as parks superintendent at Shrewsbury in 1974 he had several other occupations, each of which would have been more than enough in itself to occupy some people. Far from cutting back after his retirement, he went on accepting new commitments, such as his weekly column for the *Daily Mail* from the early spring of 1975.

In his will Percy left some £600,000. It was a considerable sum for one who had begun with virtually nothing. This wealth did not come directly from his most public activity, which was television. In 1962, for example, when he was fast rising towards the peak of his television career, his earnings from the BBC were precisely £1,350, which included a fee of £30 for a guest appearance on the *Benny Hill Show*. Ten years later his fees for a two-programme recording session for *Gardeners' World* at The Magnolias were around £500 for the use of the garden and £500 for his own contributions. When he left the programme in 1976 the last thing he needed was money, yet his work schedule was as full as ever.

One of the first jobs of these years was writing his memoirs (*My Lifetime of Gardening*, published by Hamlyn in 1977) compiled with the assistance of Ronald Webber. The book amounts to a review of the changing fashions in gardening that Percy had seen and frequently been part of. The theme was a favourite one, in conversation, articles and in lectures.

Among Percy's greatest gifts, and a particularly engaging one, was the ability to be himself and to behave in the same way without regard to the company he was in. It was true of his style of lecturing, which never changed, except in the degree of aplomb, from the day he had spoken to the Townswomen's Guild in Derby. In later years the subject seldom changed either, whether his audience was made up of professionals or amateurs, the young or the old, an allotment society or a women's institute. It was the subject he chose when invited to address a fairly high-powered audience at the Royal Institution, which has been described by its then director, Sir George Porter, as 'London's repertory company of science'.

Percy's discourse was part of a series in which he appeared between two fellows of the Royal Society, on Friday 13 March 1976, a time of tension in his life because the row with the BBC over his television advertisements for ICI was about to reach its crisis. Unperturbed, and pressed at the last minute into a dinner-jacket, he proceeded to speak after a good dinner. The lecture was his trusted one, tried and proved with many audiences over many years: 'Changing Fashions in Gardening'.

The lecture began with the point that gardening was high on the list of the nation's hobbies and was possibly number one. It provided a sense of achievement, relaxation, peace of mind and relief from the pressures of life. He deplored the decline and virtual disappearance of large gardens on private estates because of taxation because these had been the training grounds of gardeners. Nevertheless, there were perhaps thirteen million people in this country with some sort of garden and between them they regularly spent about £150 million a year on them. The horticultural trade had changed with gardens and gardeners. Garden centres had become the main sources of supply for plant material, and there was a growing preference for planting permanent subjects, such as roses, trees, shrubs and hardy perennial plants. While the initial cost of planting a garden in this way was probably greater than the more labour intensive gardens of the past, with their emphasis on bedding plants and other annuals, there was probably a saving of time and money in the longer term by following the new style. In the climate of the times, the garden must never be allowed to become a burden; if it does, it will be neglected.

This speech went down just as well with the relatively sophisticated audience in the Royal Institution as it had done with perhaps less demanding listeners in village halls up and down the country. The ability to communicate effectively at many different levels was a matter of private envy among some of Percy's peers at the top of his profession. The Royal Horticultural Society had made him an Associate of Honour – an award for people who had 'rendered distinguished service to horticulture in the course of their employment' – in 1962. In 1973 came the Society's top award, the Victoria Medal of Honour – whose number never exceed sixty-three, that being the number of years in Queen Victoria's reign – which had scarcely ever been given to the 'other ranks', that is to say those who gardened for a living. Thus Charles Cook, for example, who had spent his entire working life as a gardener and achieved tremendous distinction as a gardener, did not receive his profession's top accolade. Percy's pleasure and

141

pride in his VMH can be imagined; but he admitted that the award caused him to ponder the lifteime's good fortune that had led him to it.

There were other awards, including the MBE in 1984, and various plants named after him. The best known of them is the Hybrid tea rose 'Percy Thrower', a slightly scented pink rose, raised by Lens in Belgium from 'La Jolla' and 'Karl Herbst', and introduced in this country in 1964 by Gregorys of Nottingham, who were old friends of both Percy and the Shrewsbury Flower Show. The bush has a tendency to sprawl, but the flowers, when cut in bud, are exceptionally long-lasting which has made it popular with flower arrangers.

The most rewarding job of Percy's later years was back on television, with a place on the children's programme *Blue Peter*. His audience could well have been largely made up of the grandchildren of the generation whom he had first enthused for gardening on the BBC. Broadcasting to children was by no means new to him when he joined *Blue Peter*, however.

In February 1950 Percy had started giving monthly ten-minute talks on the BBC Midland Region edition of *Children's Hour* in a series called 'Our Garden'. Part of the intention was the simple one of introducing a new generation to gardening; another aim was an attempt to discourage vandalism by children in public parks by giving them some knowledge of plants and the chance to participate in gardening. In Shrewsbury, four local boys and four local girls began cultivating a special border in the Quarry, given mainly to annuals grown from seed. Similar projects were set up in parks in other towns within the Midland Region, which in those days ranged from Gloucester to Great Yarmouth and from Northampton to Derby, with Percy doing programmes from all of them in rotation. The venture was given a little edge by the introduction of an 'Our Garden' show from Birmingham. All of Percy's daughters were lined up to take part when their time came, although the extent to which the will to garden took root in them varied hugely.

Percy became *Blue Peter*'s gardener after he retired from Shrewsbury in 1974 and his appearances continued after he had left *Gardener's World* in 1976. The *Blue Peter* garden was originally just a plot measuring twelve feet by ten feet behind the Television Centre in Wood Lane, West London, where efforts at planting and cultivation were frequently menaced and sometimes undone by the programme's dog, 'Shep'. Percy made over two hundred broadcasts from this garden and became one of the programme's most valued props. Just as his audience at the Royal Institution could only respond to the copper-bottomed authenticity of the man, so children responded most enthusiastically to his grandfatherly presence and sense of humour.

The practical jokes beloved of the film crews on *Gardening Club* and *Gardeners' World* followed him on to *Blue Peter*. A model of 'Britain's head gardener' had been on display at Madame Tussauds for some years. Percy well remembered the day at The Magnolias when two girls from the waxworks had measured him up and matched him to the remarkable collection of glass eyes and false hair which they brought with them. Though he had an open invitation to go and look at himself at the waxworks in Baker Street, years passed and he had never done so. Arriving at the BBC one day for a *Blue Peter* programme he was told to expect a small surprise on the set. He walked into the *Blue Peter* garden to find John Noakes, then the programme's presenter, addressing a life-size model of himself, complete with muddy shoes, watering can and pipe. Noakes was saying: 'Hello, Percy, what do you think of the garden then? Eh? . . . It's not so bad as all that, is it? I think he's speechless!' At which Percy stepped in and said: '*He* might be . . . but *I'm* not!'

His fan mail equalled that of many of the children's more obvious idols. His last editor on the programme, Biddy Baxter, confidently asserted in her postscript to his obituary in *The Times* that 'his enthusiasm and expertise inspired a whole new generation of gardeners'.

Inspiring a new generation of gardeners was, as so much of Percy's public career had been, basic spadework fuelling a huge and ever-growing leisure industry. Percy could tell people how to make a bit of paradise out of an unpromising backyard using the methods which his father might have employed in making the gardens at Horwood. But these new gardeners, once they had seen the prospect of beauty in a dismal scene, were disinclined to wait. Having glimpsed paradise, they wanted their bit of it now.

One essential development towards fulfilling these dreams was the appearance in this country in the early 1960s of garden centres, where everything necessary to the garden could be seen displayed and tried-out, and taken home there and then, the shrubs very probably in bloom. For those in a hurry the days when haste was inimical to good gardening were numbered. There was no longer any need to nurture a cutting before it was ready to be placed in its permanent position – which in the case of a tree might be several years. A container-grown azalea, for example, seen in brilliant flower one afternoon in a garden centre could be removed and reinstated, still blooming, outside the kitchen window that evening. Although widely deplored, container growing and the flexibility it gives over planting times has many advantages, most of all the freedom to plant at the best moment, for during the traditional planting season of November to March the soil is often at its least receptive.

In later years Percy spent many days away from home opening new garden centres and thus endorsing them by his presence. His own garden centre at Shrewsbury was his main preoccupation when officially retired. His introduction to garden centres went back to their earliest days in this country and came as a result of his work for ICI. In 1967 ICI asked Percy for his advice prior to setting up a horticultural exhibition and garden centre at Syon Park, the Duke of Northumberland's house in West London, facing Kew across the Thames. The 1960s were one of the bleakest periods for the owners of great houses and the park at Syon was slightly run down. Capability Brown's foundations for the park were sound enough, but the lake was clogged and, owing to variations in the level of the river, minor flooding was an occasional risk. Some landscape work was thus necessary before building the exhibition and centre on the site of fifty acres which ICI leased from the Duke. The natural qualities of the site made it suitable for establishing examples of different sorts of garden, and the vast Conservatory was ideal for the house-plant side, as well as for machinery and other garden aids. The centre was opened by the Queen Mother in June 1968. The exhibition continued for five years and the present garden centre at Syon followed in other hands.

Although well tuned to the Shrewsbury grape-vine, Percy was away in Edinburgh opening a new garden centre for Waterers in 1970 when he heard that the celebrated firm of Murrells of Shrewsbury was up for sale. The firm was known particularly to fastidious rose growers, for it was one of the half dozen serious growers of 'old' roses in this country. It was known to Percy as a valued supplier. Edwin Murrell had supplied some of the seed from which the new turf in the Quarry was sown after the war. Members of the family, especially Hilda Murrell, who was to be the victim of a particularly gruesome and still unsolved murder, were old friends.

Percy was no entrepreneur when it came to investing money. It was not an instinct that would naturally appear in one who was essentially cautious, dependent for his place and success on experience, and never endowed with money beyond what he earned. But back from Edinburgh he called on his accountant, Doug Whittingham, to find out more about the position over Murrells. Percy had assumed that one of the large established firms of nurserymen, such as Waterers, would acquire Murrells; but Whittingham informed him that the strongest interest so far was from another Shrewsbury man, Duncan Murphy, who had just sold his family's Wrekin Brewery and thus found himself with money ready to be put to work. The result was a sensible marriage of money and expertise, in the purchase of Murrells by Murphy and Percy in partnership, with the greater part of the money coming from Murphy.

The site of the new garden centre on the A5 Shrewsbury ring road was an excellent one for the largely motor-borne trade. Apart from the Shrewsbury area itself, its catchment included a wide slice of the West Midlands from where it could be agreeably accessible on a Sunday afternoon. Just up the road there was also the new town of Telford, with all its back gardens waiting to be planted up. Access to the centre from the ring road was improved; and any surprised by the sign 'Percy Thrower's Gardening Centre' could easily double back at the next roundabout.

Percy himself was often there, particularly in the days when the various methods of cultivation and preparation for sale were going through the teething phase. Later, when the institution had developed a way of life of its own, Percy admitted to an enjoyable *frisson* as the staff jumped to it when he walked in unexpectedly, just as, when a young improver, he had bent to his work when Charles Cook's tread disturbed the gravel in the gardens at Windsor. To customers he was welcoming and attentive. Mrs Joan Garton, a fairly regular visitor from nearby, remembers that 'he would carry the heavier purchases to one's car himself, rather than calling one of his staff'. Another from further afield, Mrs Durrant, was surprised when she expressed an interest in his show fuchsias which were kept in a locked greenhouse that he insisted on going off to find a key so that he could show them to her. Latterly, following Duncan Murphy's departure from the partnership, the centre has been run by Percy's daughters with a full-time staff of fourteen.

The garden centre was an example of the impact of television on gardening at one extreme: fulfilling the dreams that had become possibilities in the hands of Percy and his successors among the television impresarios of gardening. Television, too, had a part in broadening the horizons of gardeners in a very literal sense, in inspiring the desire to see for themselves the exotic flora which can never thrive outdoors in this country, if indeed they will take root away from their native soil at all.

The idea of travelling to see tropical and other plants was as attractive a novelty to Percy as to anyone else, for since his visit to Berlin he remained one of the world's least travelled men. The greatest attraction of all was that Connie would go with him on many of the excursions. The cruises became a succession of second honeymoons, free of the dangers that had overhung their early married life, where they had more time to enjoy one another's company than during most of the intervening years.

The scheme was put to him by two Shrewsbury travel agents, Harold Sleigh and Brian Bass, in the early 1960s and, as with the garden centre, it involved an investment of Percy's own money. The earlier tours were relatively unambitious, principally four-day jaunts to Holland, but presently grew to longer and more expensive cruises to the Caribbean or South Africa. The prospect of being locked up on a ship with a body of gardening fanatics might not have appealed to all gardeners, and indeed the cruises had their social hazards. Some of the parties of people flying out to join the cruises would be old ladies who might never have been abroad before – at least, certainly not by air – and so they were bracing themselves for the unknown as Percy had done on that stormy evening at Northolt in 1951. For reasons that Percy well understood, delays on the ground increased their nervousness. A half hour's delay called for a glass of brandy on the firm (that is to say a free drink on Percy and his partners); a further half hour demanded another glass or so; a two-hour delay made it impossible not to offer a full meal, with wine. These occasional drinkers had their advantages, however. Returing from Miami from one of the later excursions by air, Percy and Brian Bass found themselves provisioned with whisky in excess of the duty free allowance and spread the surplus bottles around their party while they went through customs.

At this time Percy's was one of the most recognized faces in the country; even if he was not immediately recognized, his face would cause people to grope in their memories. Although the most accessible of men, with a gift for making a

148

remembered acquaintance out of a casual encounter, his appearance could bring on a form of reverse stage fright. A party was tumbling out of a charabanc into an hotel foyer when the lift opened and Percy stepped out; the hubbub changed to the silence of thirty drawn breaths. In the setting of a cruise these inhibitions soon evaporated, however, and, far from wanting to withdraw after a day's lecturing, Percy was always entirely happy to continue informally into the night. As the popularity of gardening cruises grew, there was often more than one personality aboard; far from welcoming the relief which this load-sharer might offer, Percy privately preferred cruises where he was the sole attraction and authority.

Gardening weekends in England became increasingly prominent on his schedule at home. These weekends have mainly been designed for the better heeled end of the gardening community, usually out-of-season in places such as the Imperial Hotel at Torquay. Their intention is to consider some aspect of gardening in depth, with experts to answer questions and mix generally as well as lecture, with a visit to some notable garden in the area usually included.

It was during one of these weekends, at Hawkstone Manor in November 1987, that Percy was seriously alarmed to find that he could not perform to anything approaching his customary standard. This was the beginning of the last phase of a gradual but not generally perceived decline. In a special edition of *Gardeners' World* with Geoffrey Smith, broadcast from The Magnolias in October 1987, which proved to be valedictory, he had appeared somewhat puffy in the face but full of vigour. A succession of heart problems from 1985 had not caused him to slow down very drastically, although he had obeyed an instruction to give up his pipe – wishing, once

149

he had done so, that he had taken the step years before. He was in and out of hospital and in the course of an exploratory operation the Hodgkin's disease, which was the eventual cause of his death, was discovered. In practical terms, Connie noticed that he did not seem to want to go out much; he certainly complained of tiredness. In March 1988 he went into hospital in Shrewsbury, from where he was later removed to Wolverhampton. It was only then that he formally announced his retirement, although he managed a short recording for *Blue Peter* from hospital a week before he died, aged seventy-five, on 18 March.

'And so Percy goes from us,' said Maurice Turner, the Vicar of Bomere Heath, in his address at the funeral at St Chad's, overlooking the Quarry in Shrewsbury, 'to be replanted in the Hereafter.' Those who went to the funeral, old friends stretching right back to the Horwood days, professional colleagues and acquaintances, some of them national figures in their own right, local people and humble admirers, were surprised by the scale of the event. Not only by the packed congregation in the galleried church, but by the evidence of civil solemnity round about, the policemen and television cameras, the sightseers and crush barriers.

Such was one of Percy's personal qualities: to make any friendship seem important to the extent of being unique. If gardening is one path to happiness for life, Percy Thrower can claim to have set probably millions of people off along that path. His achievement is rightly applauded.

INDEX

Index

Aberconway, Lord, 99
African Violet, 77
aircraft, 79–80
Albert, Prince, 27–8, 42, 50
Alice, Princess, Countess of
  Athlone, 70
Allestree, 63
allotments, 61–4
  BBC garden on, 101
Alvaston Lake, 63
Amateur Gardening, 105, 112
Anne, Queen, 26
Anthurium, 39
apple trees:
  bark ringing, 137
  varieties, 14
Ascot Week, 30, 40–1
Attenborough, David, 94
Aubrey (son-in-law), 111
Austen, Jane: quotation, 8
Aylesbury, Buckinghamshire,
  2

Barford, Jimmy, 9
bark ringing, 137
Baseley, Godfrey, 89–91, 92, 93,
  94, 96
Bass, Brian, 148
Bawdsey Manor, Suffolk, 5
Baxter, Biddy, 144
BBC:
  association with, 121–3
  fees, 139
  impartiality, 122
  radio, 86–93, 142–3

television, 93–101, 114, 125,
  142–4
Begonia, 121
Benny Hill Show, 139
Berlin:
  English garden, 79–82
  Tiergarten, 50, 80
Betjeman, John: quotation, 46
Beyond the Back Door, 90, 93
Billerey, 3, 5
Billitt, Arthur, 86, 117–18, 119, 122
birds: for eating, 22
Blow, Detmar, 3–4, 5
Blue Peter, 142, 143–4, 150
Bodnant, 99
Bolus, Mr, 100
bone meal, 18
Boots Company, 85–6, 117
bothy, 31–2
bothy boys:
  communal life, 31–2
  with girls, 37
Bourne, Major General G. K., 79
Bowes Lyon, Sir David, 33
Brassicas, 17–18
Brown, 'Capability', 47, 73, 145
Buccleuch, Duke of, 29
Buckinghamshire, 1–2

Cadbury family, 29
Cardiocrinum giganteum, 14
cardoon, 19
Carters, 81
Castle Kennedy, Galloway, 13–14,
  45

153

157